MW01537574

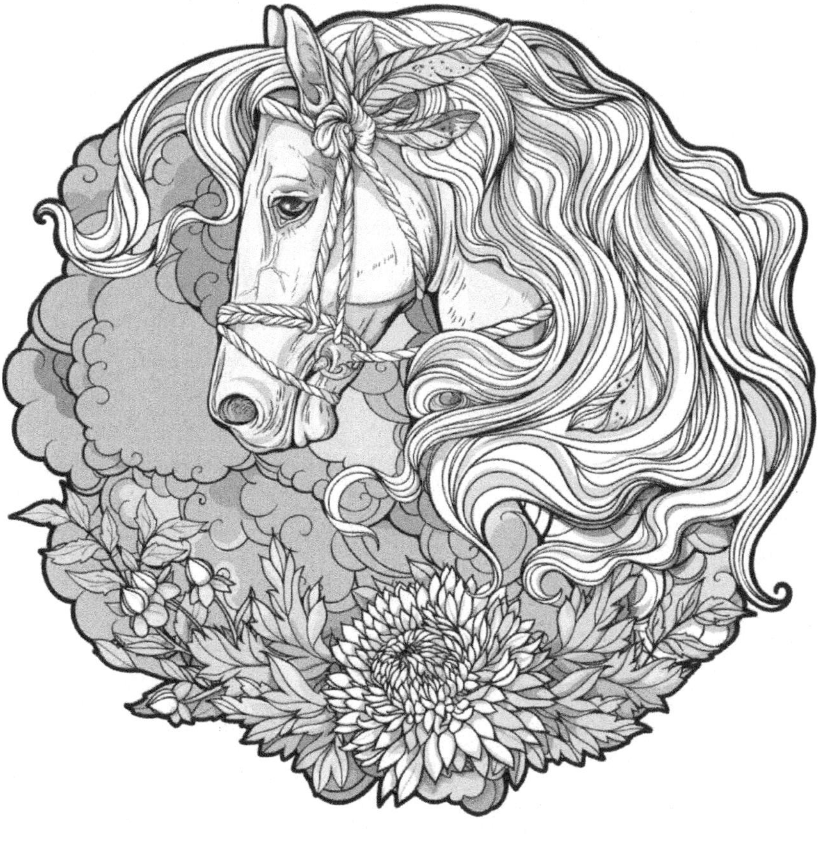

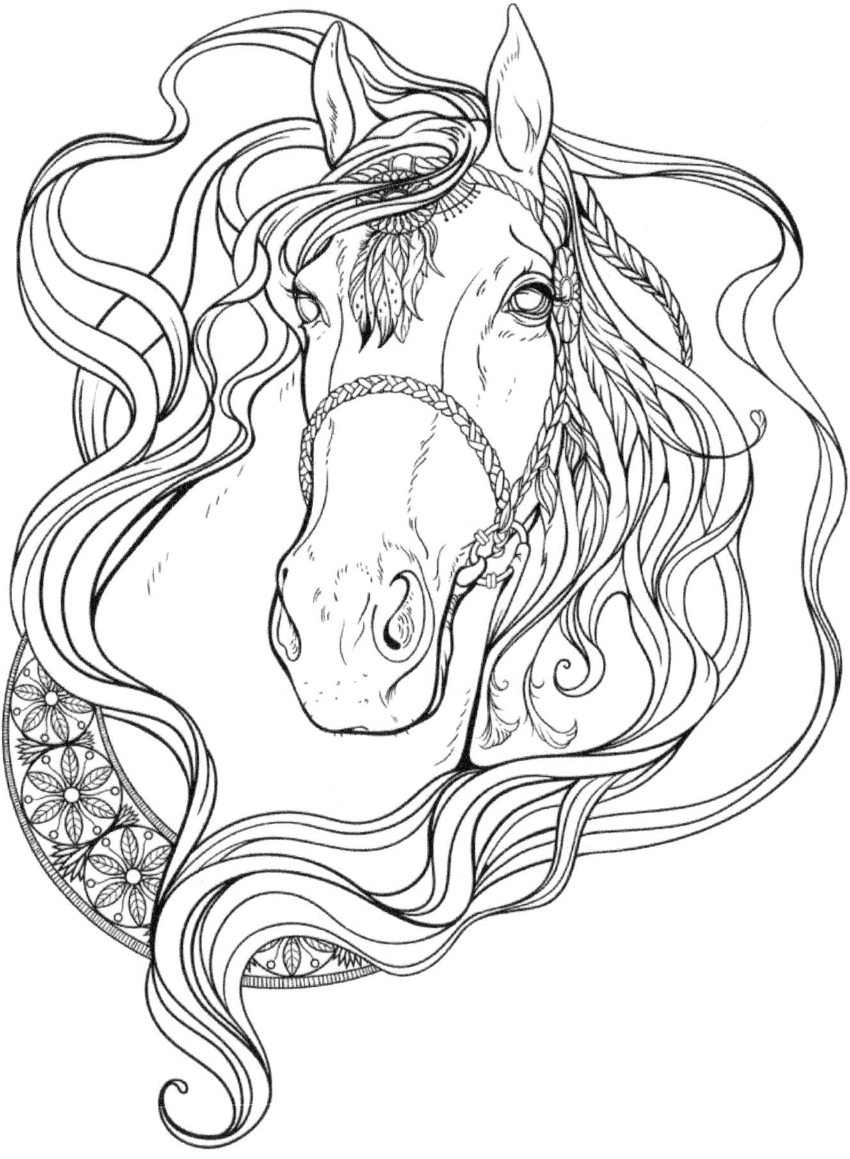

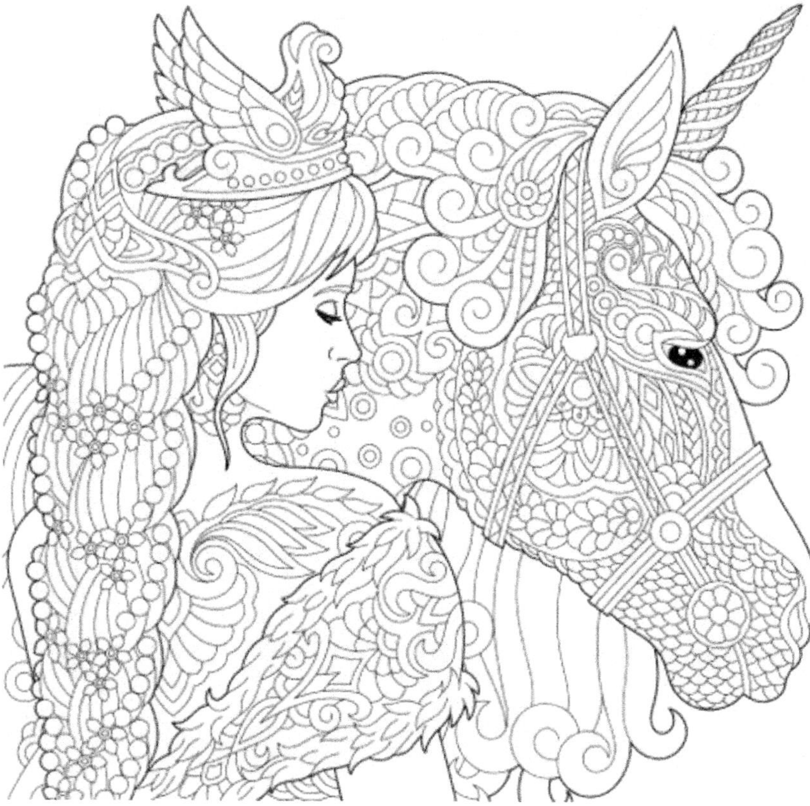

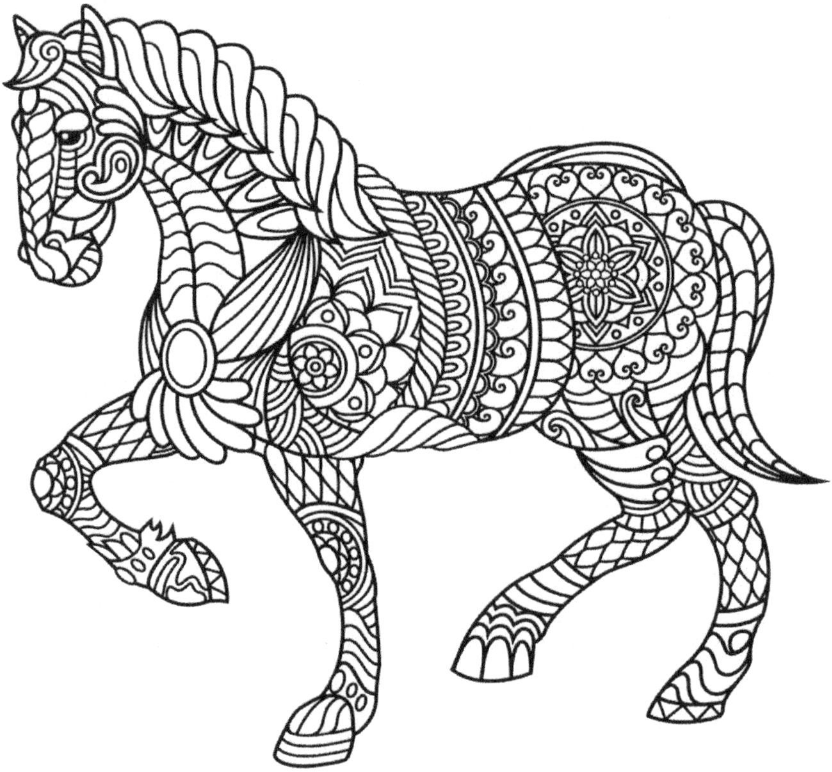

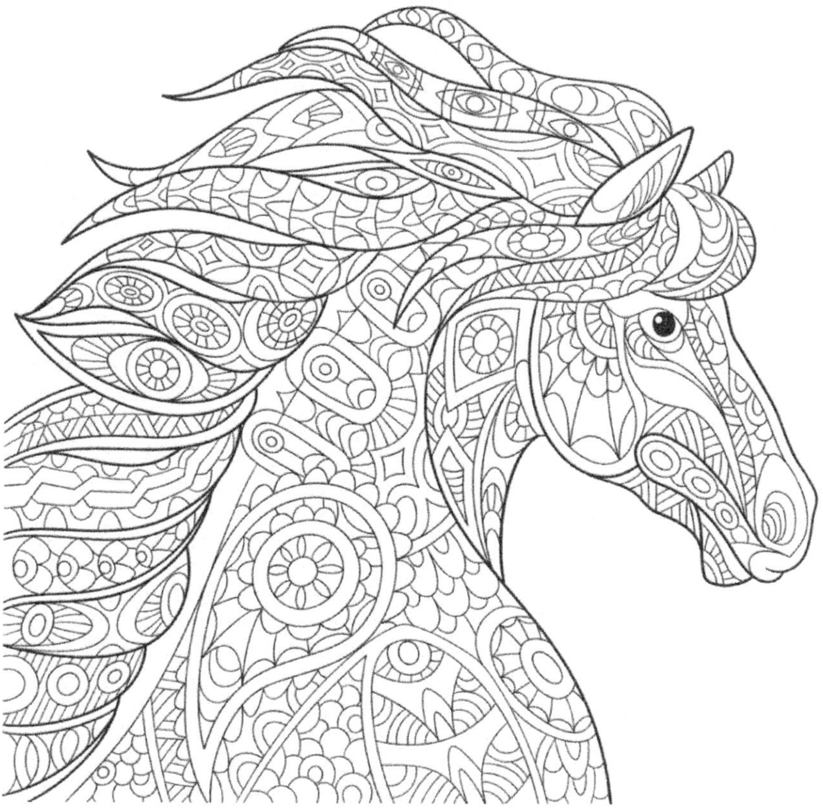

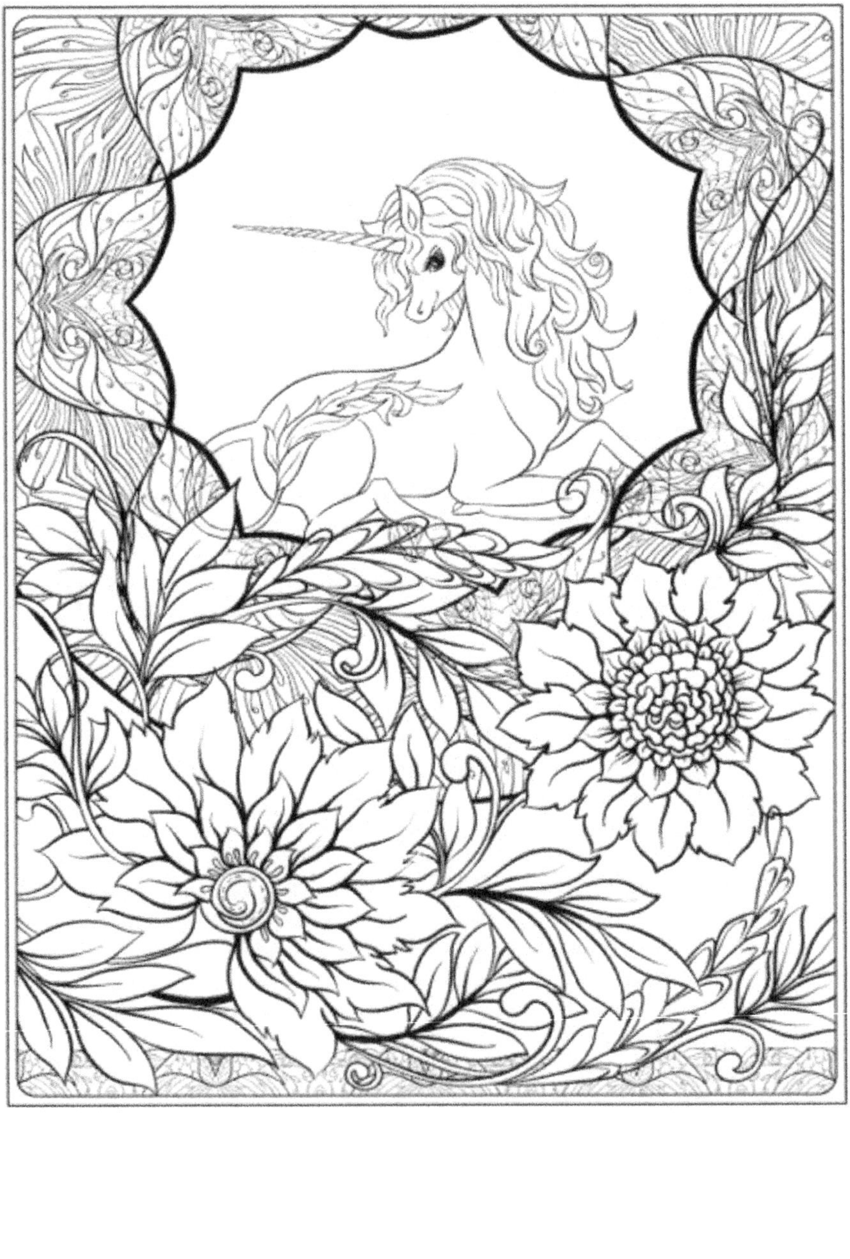

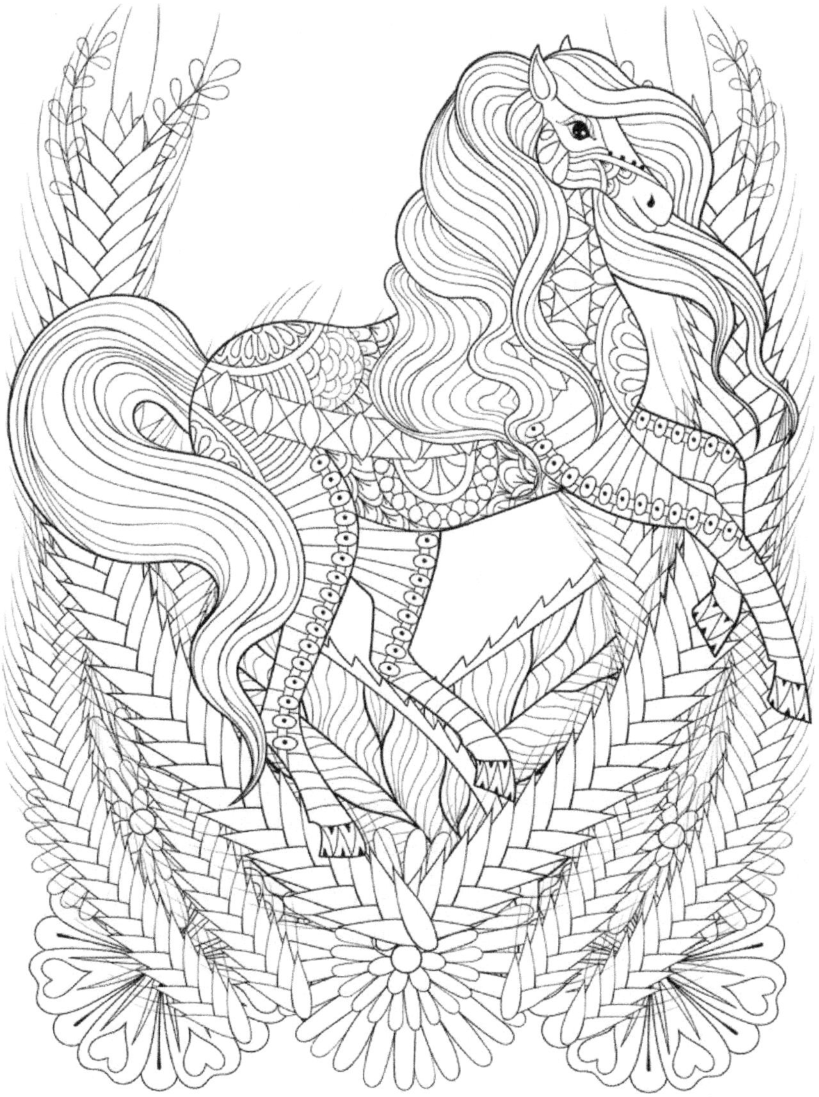

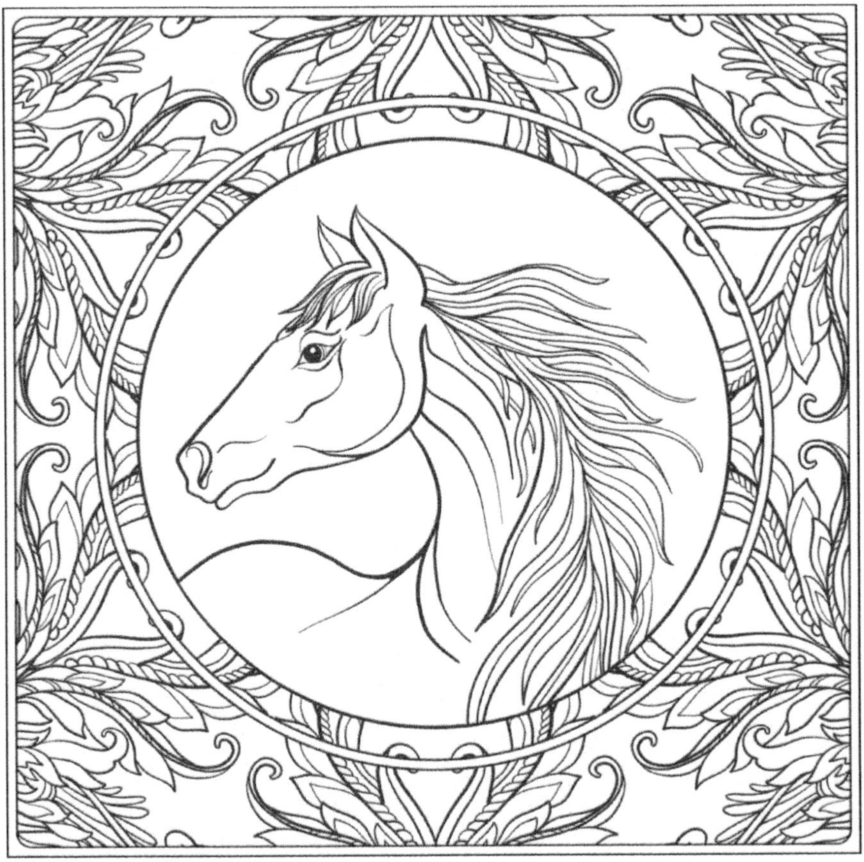

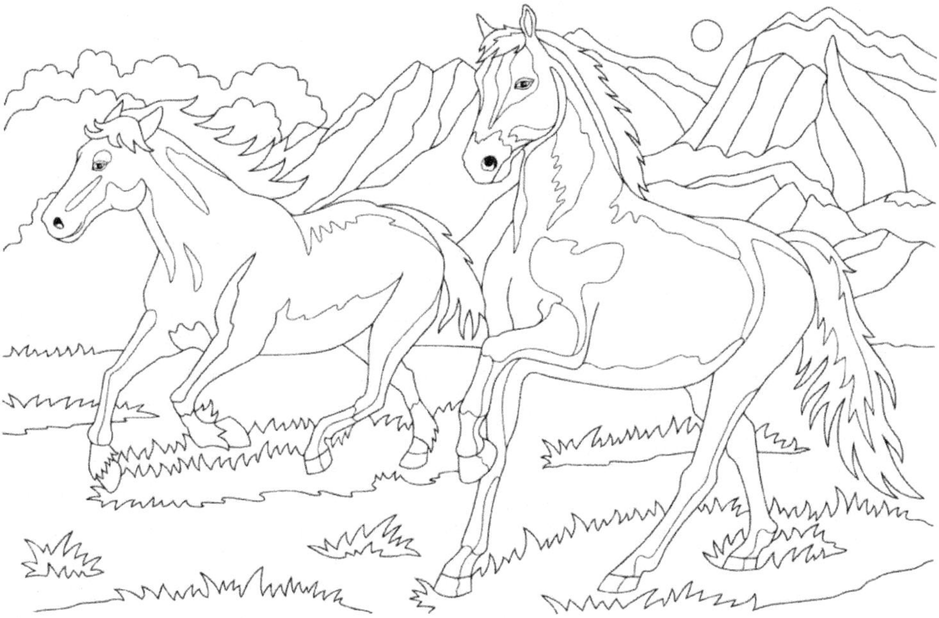

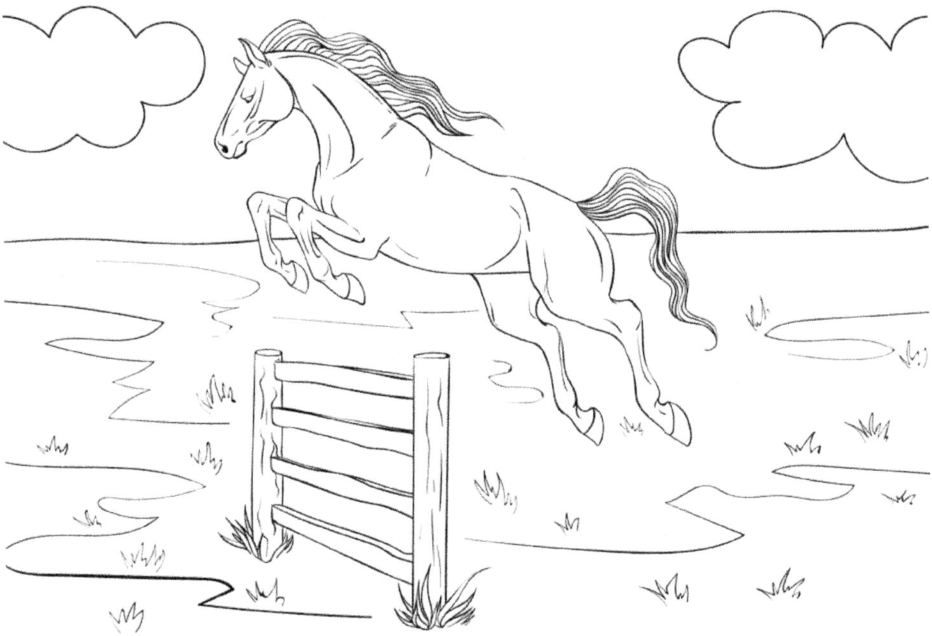

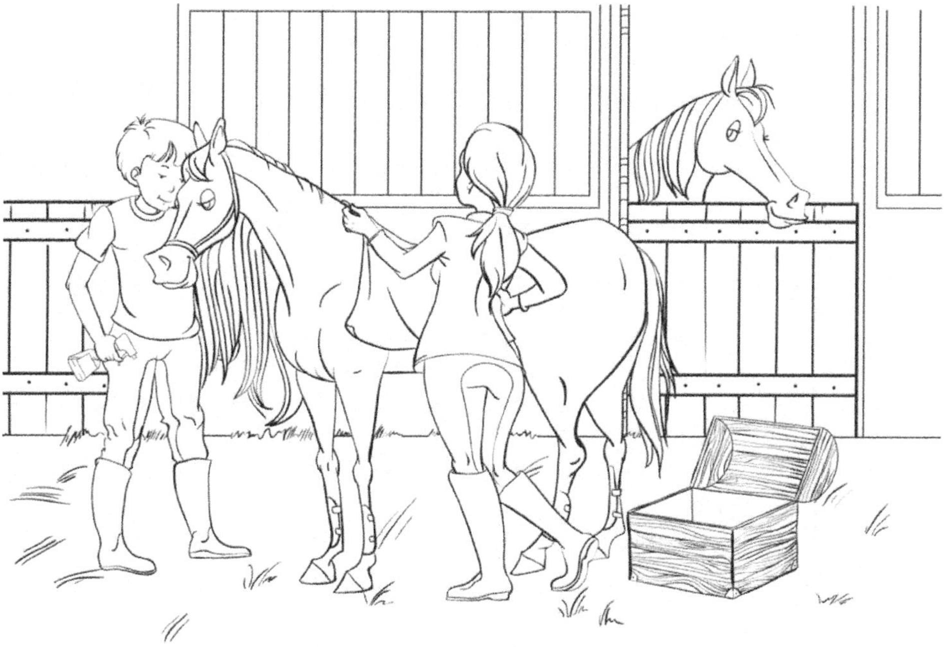

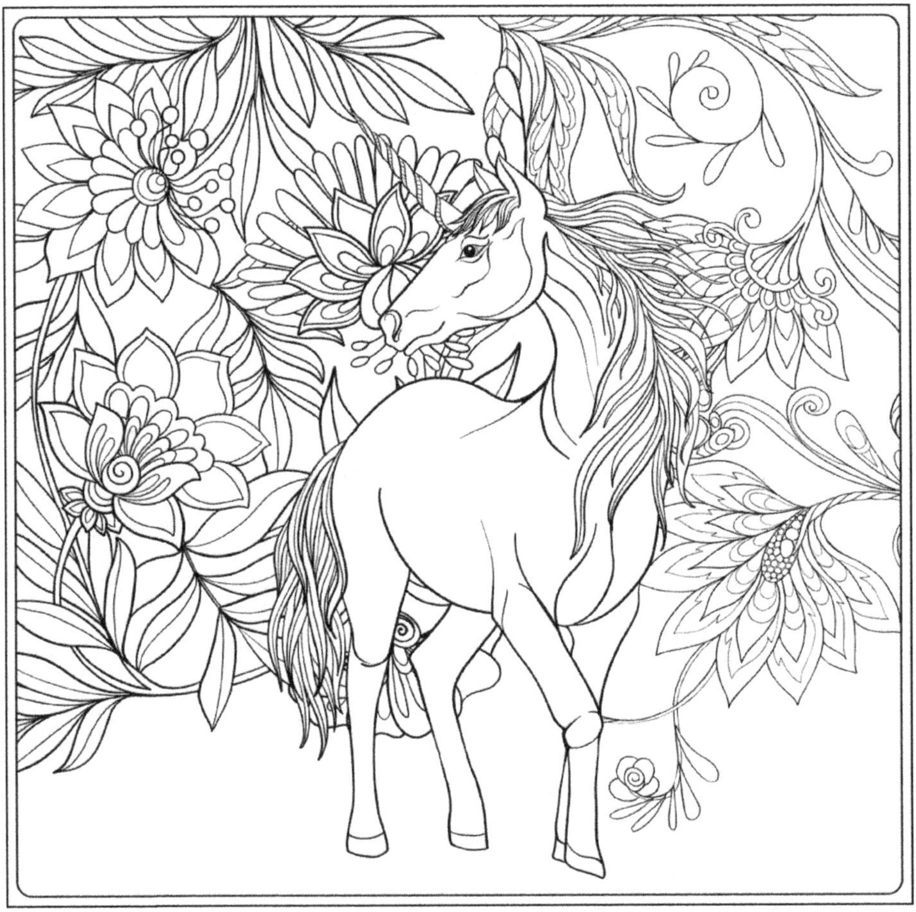

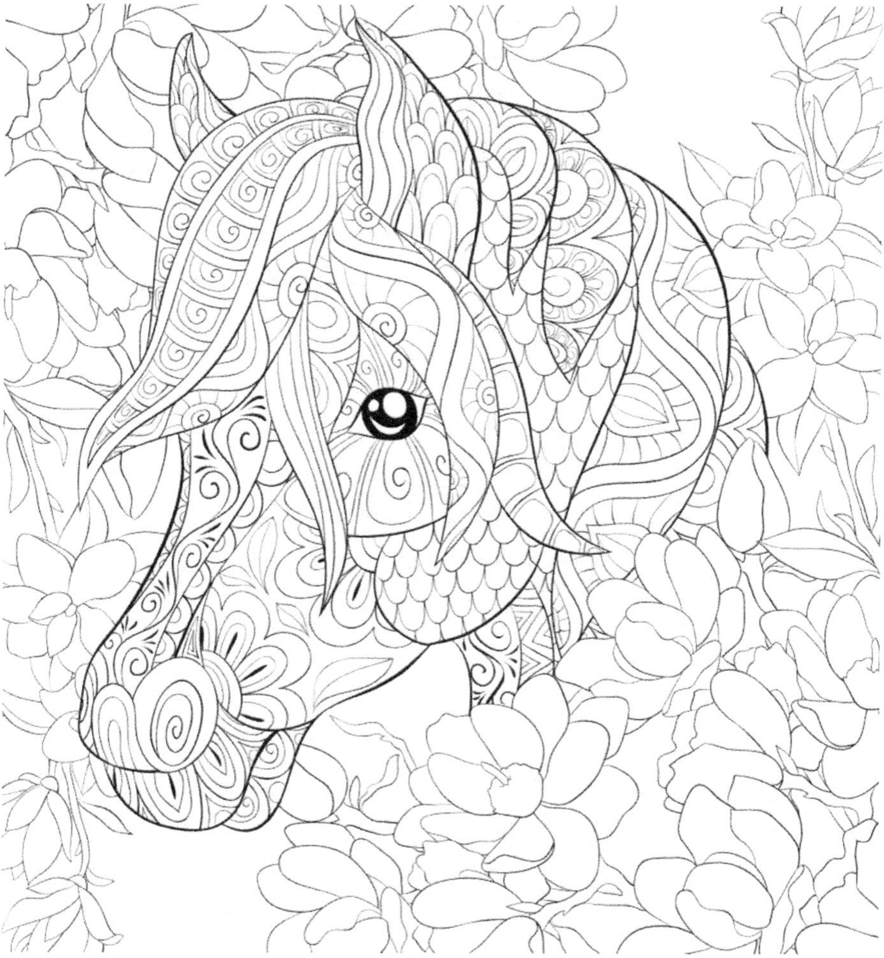

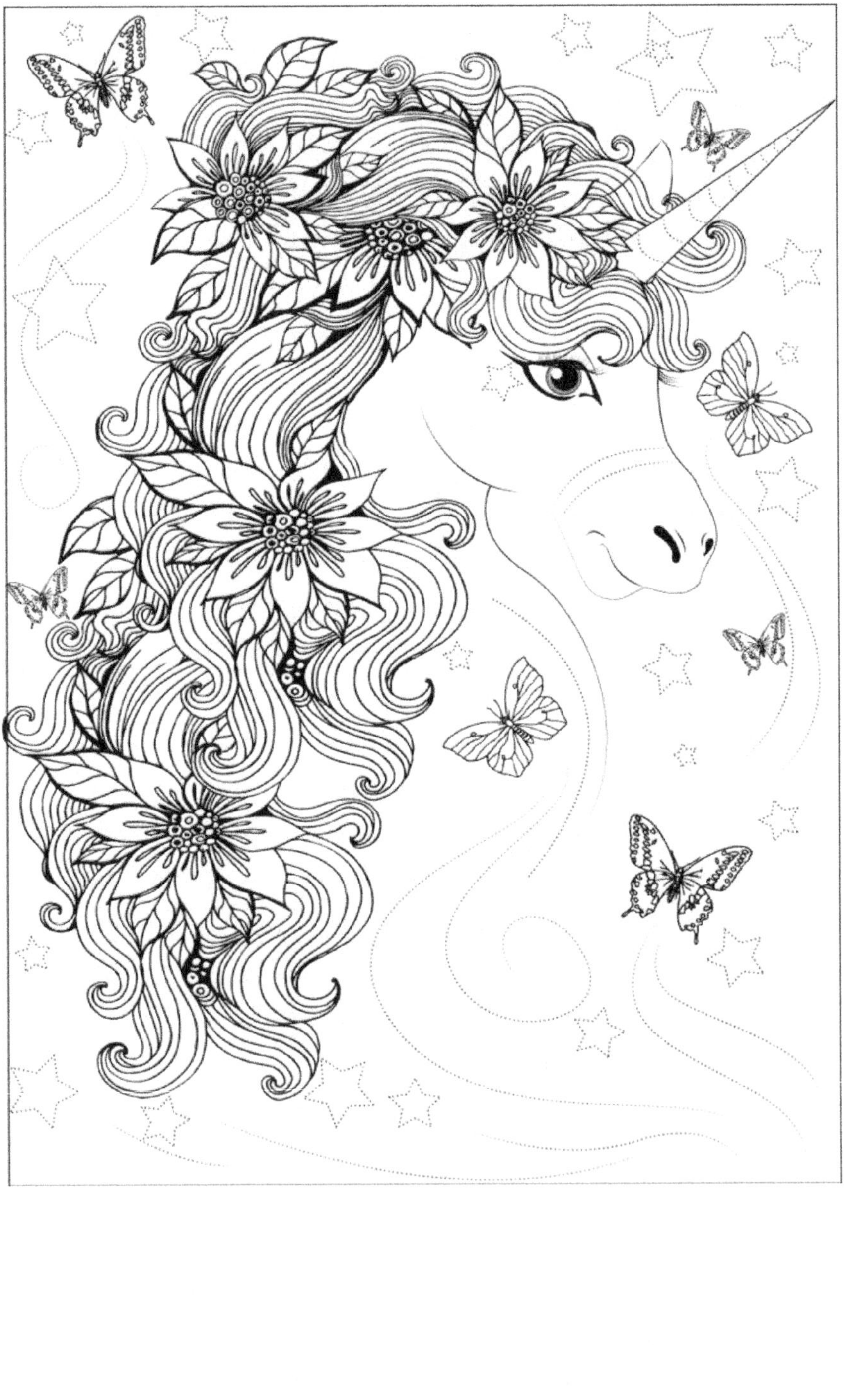

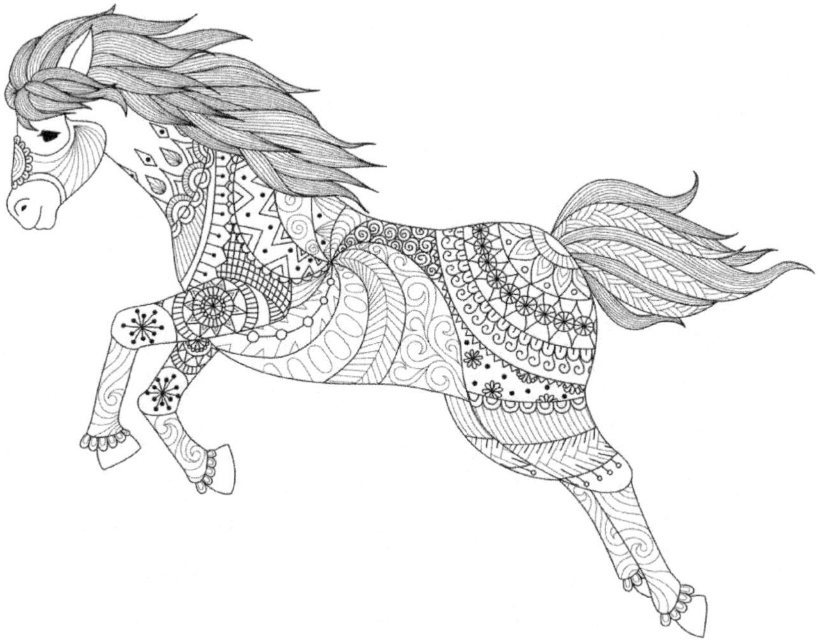

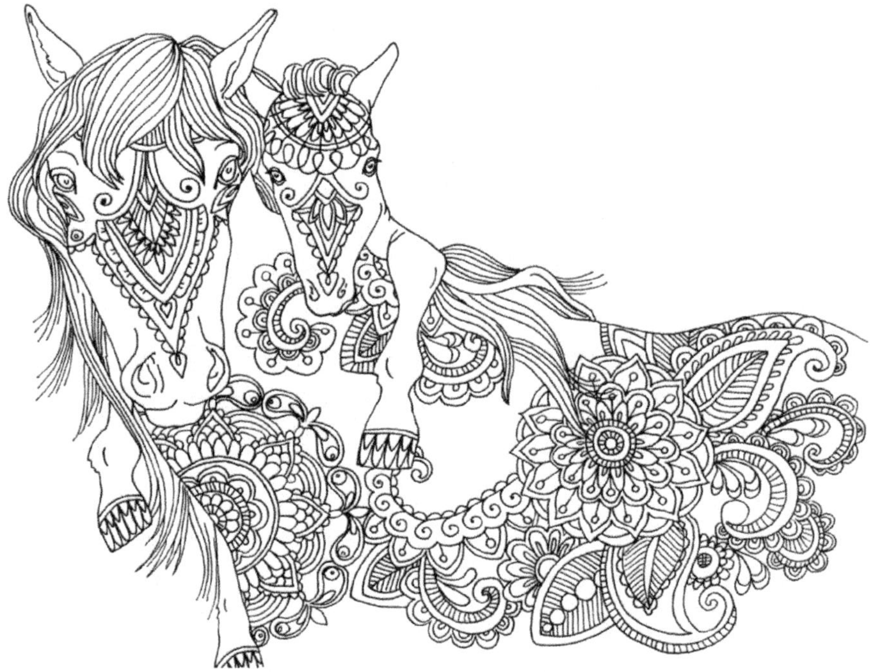

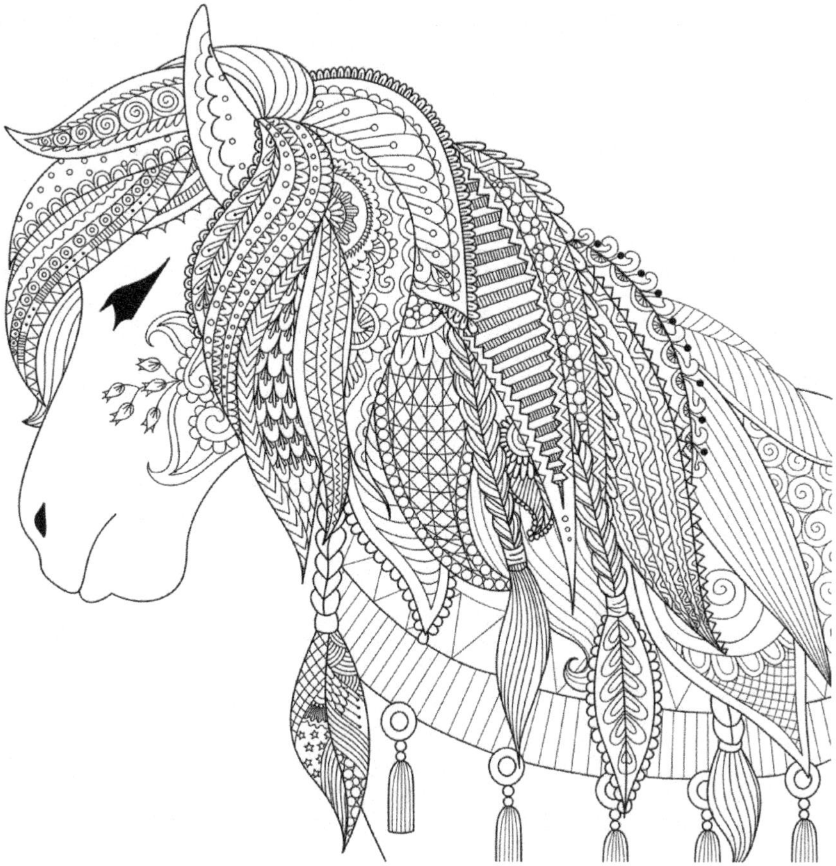

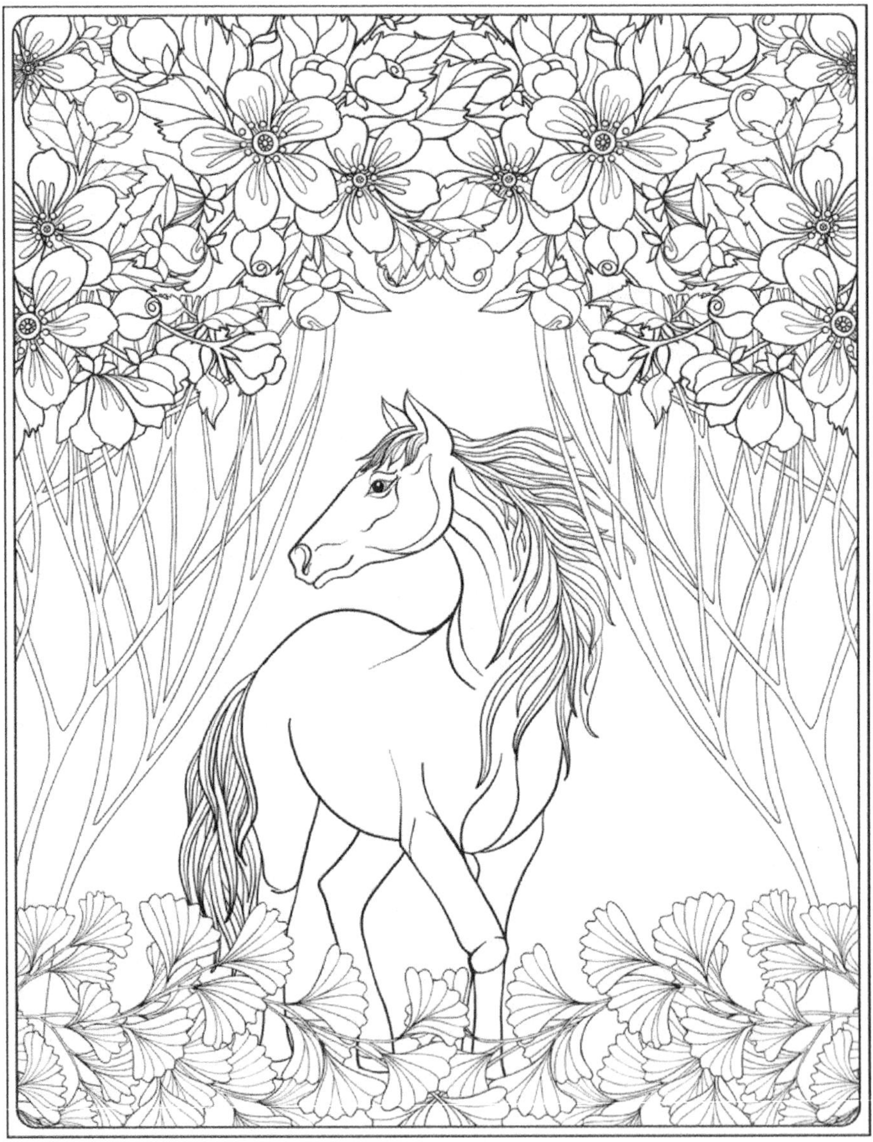

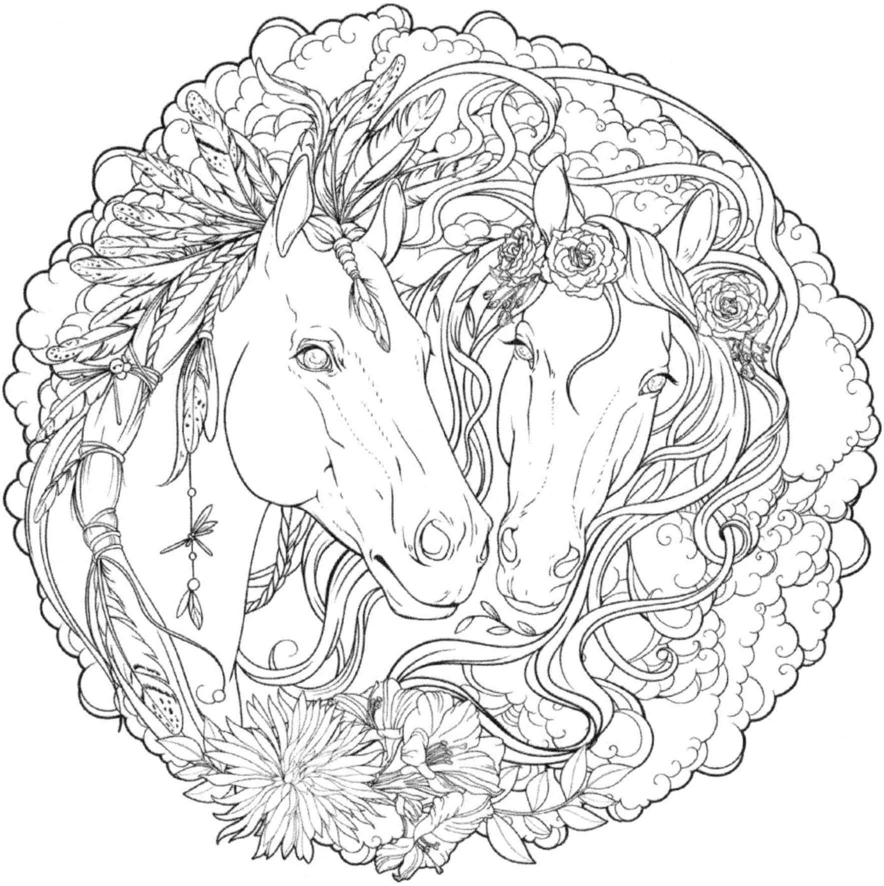

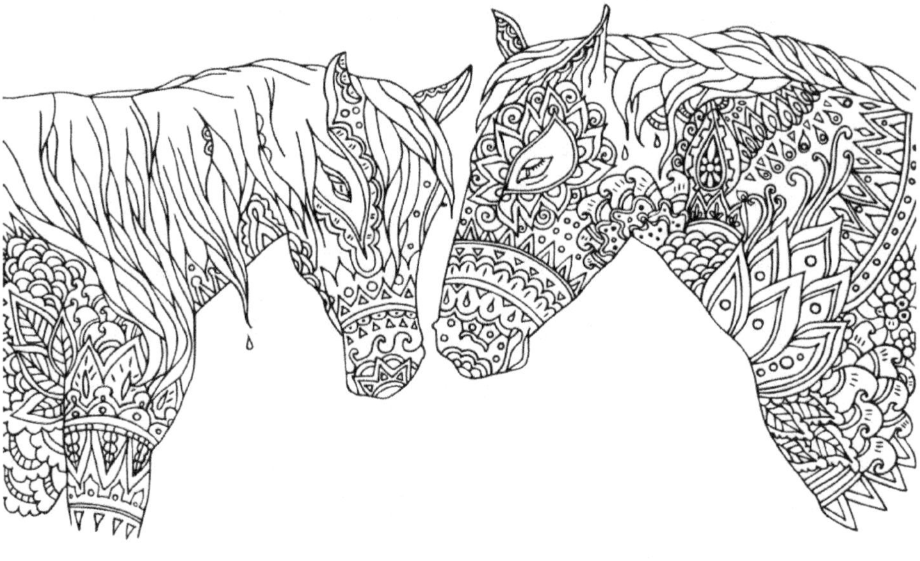

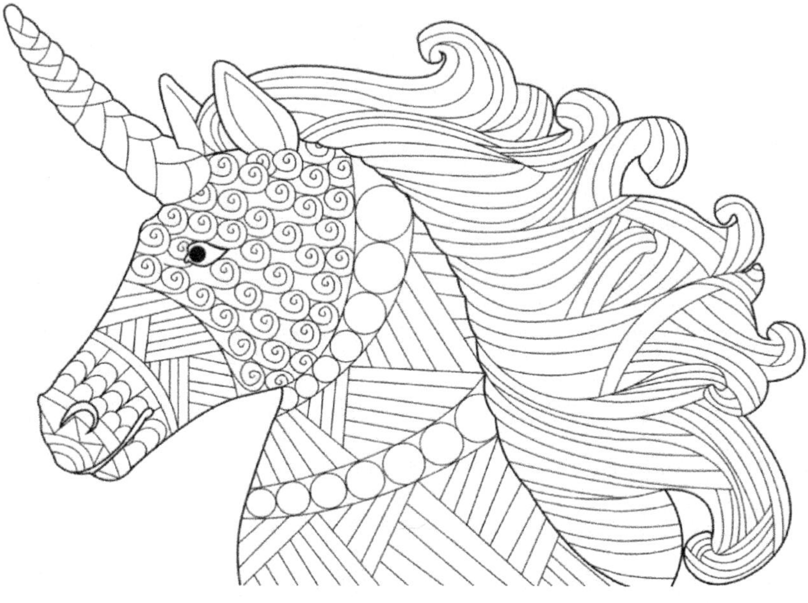

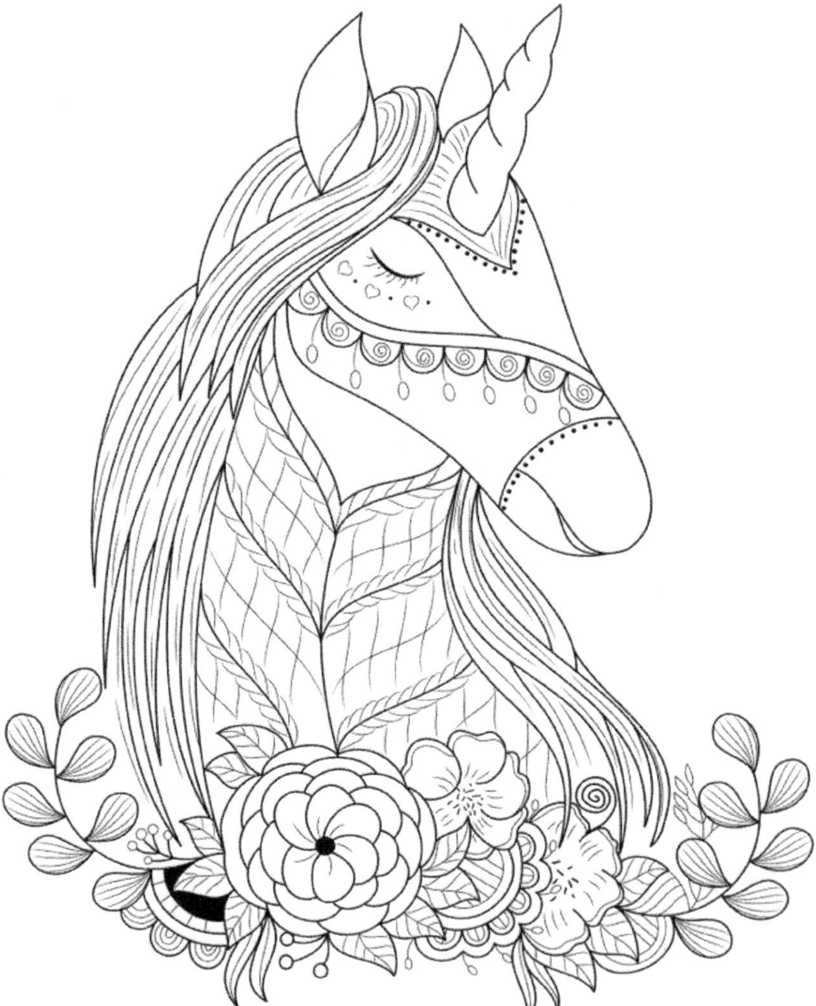

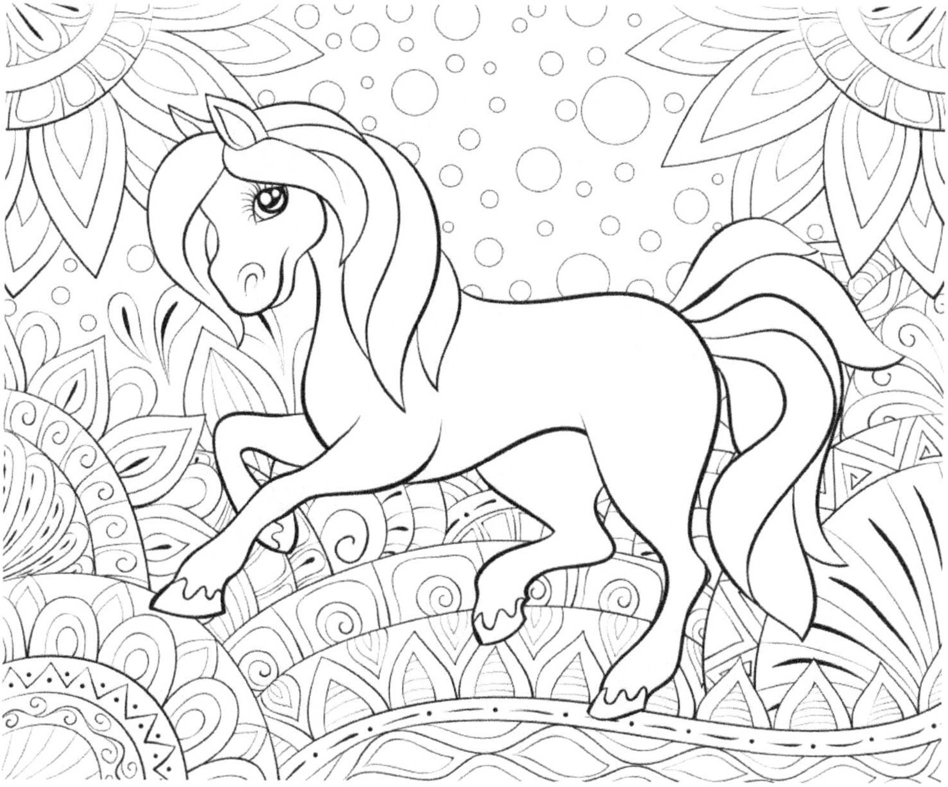

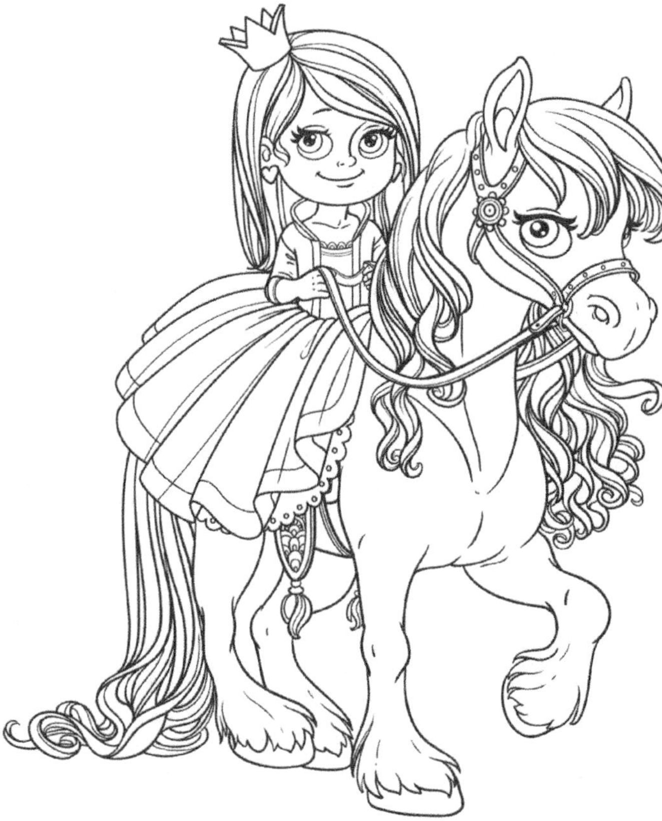

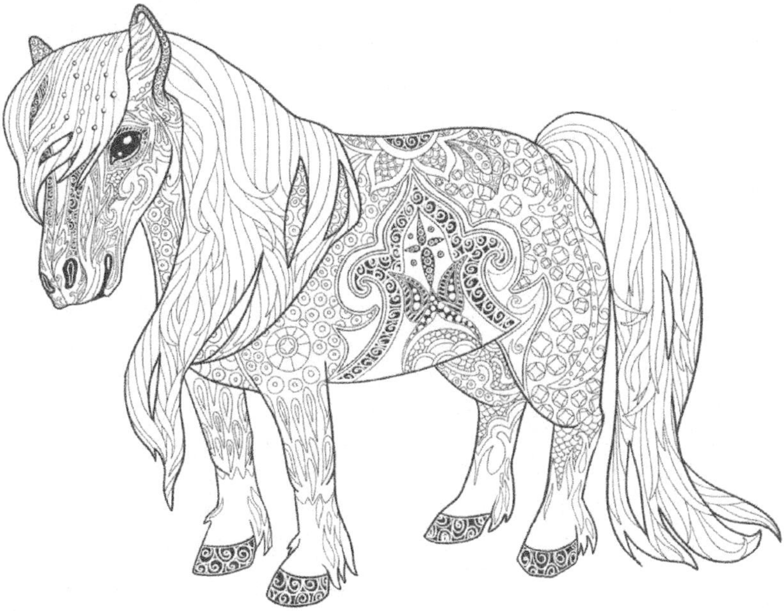

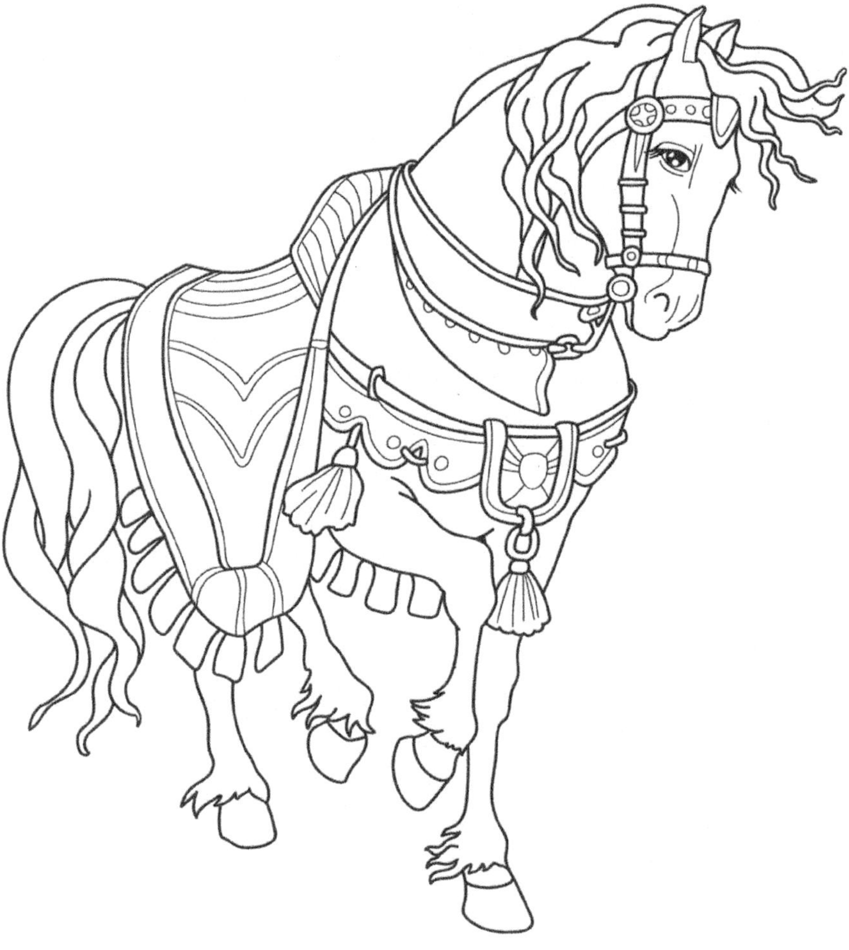

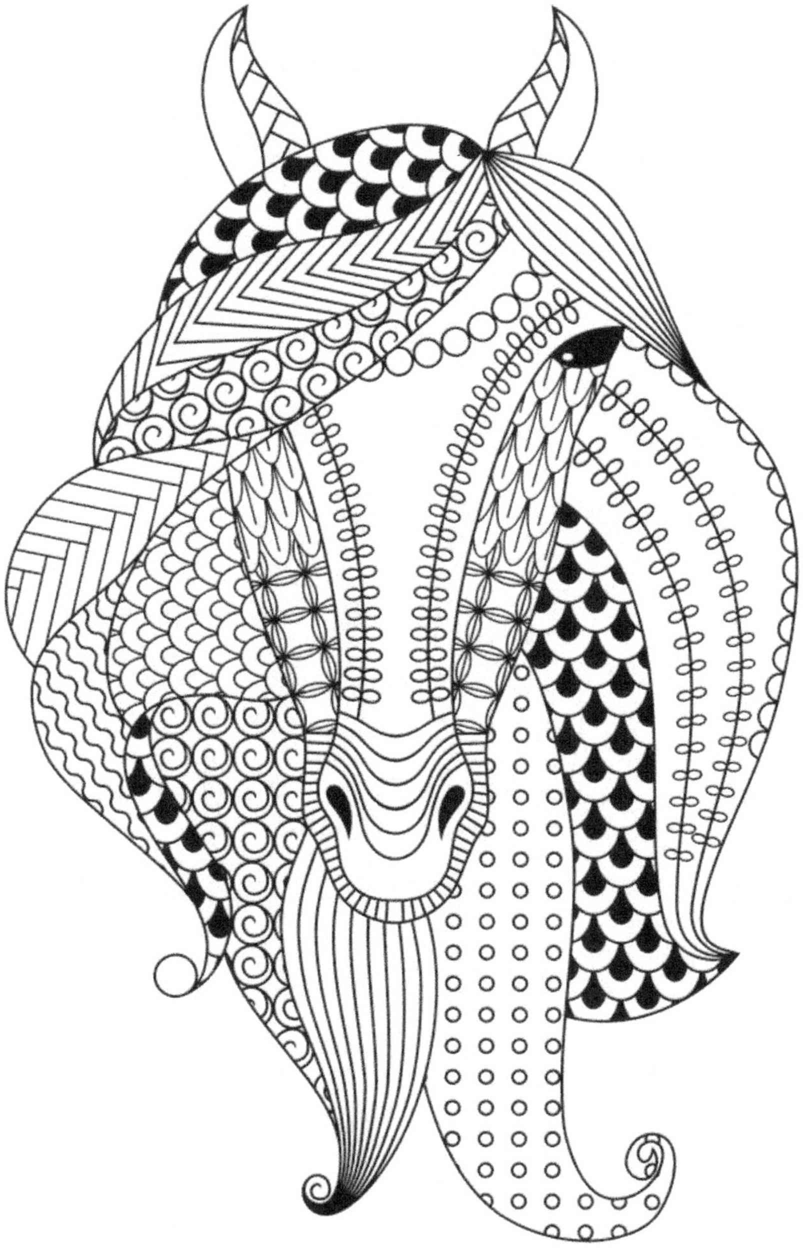

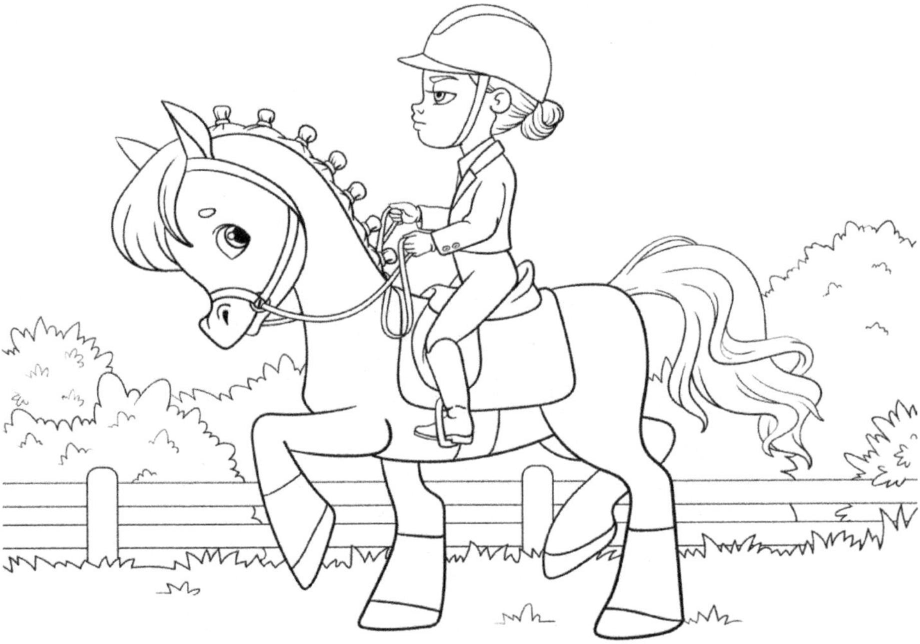

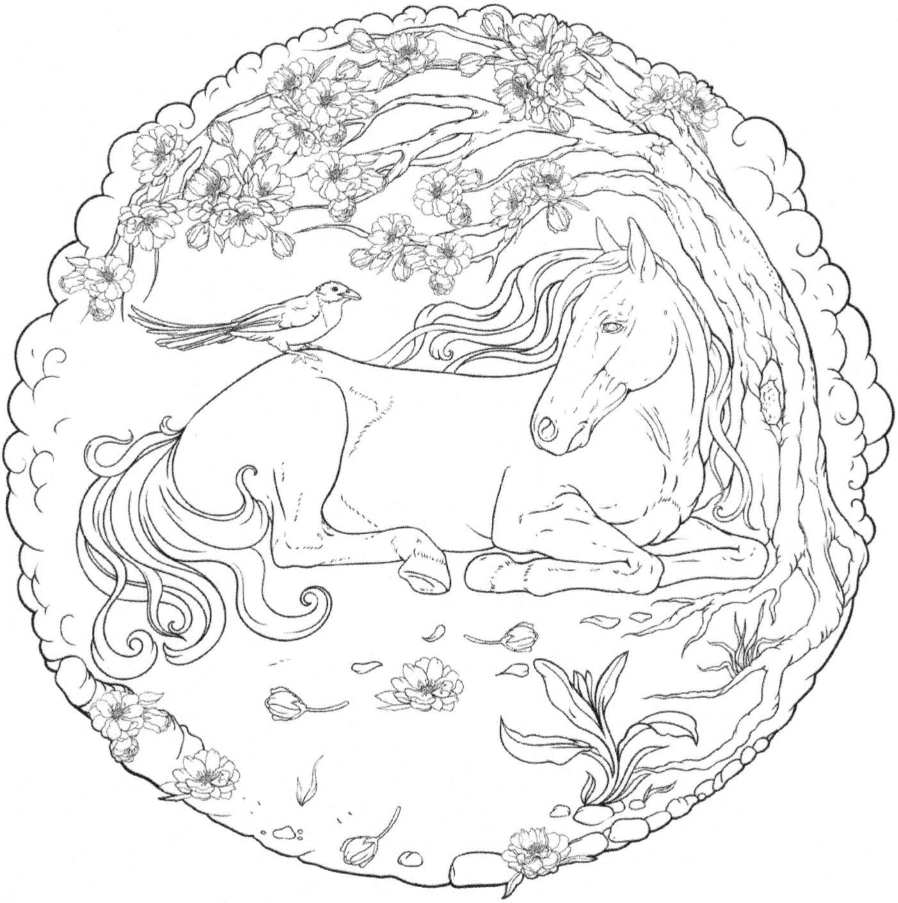

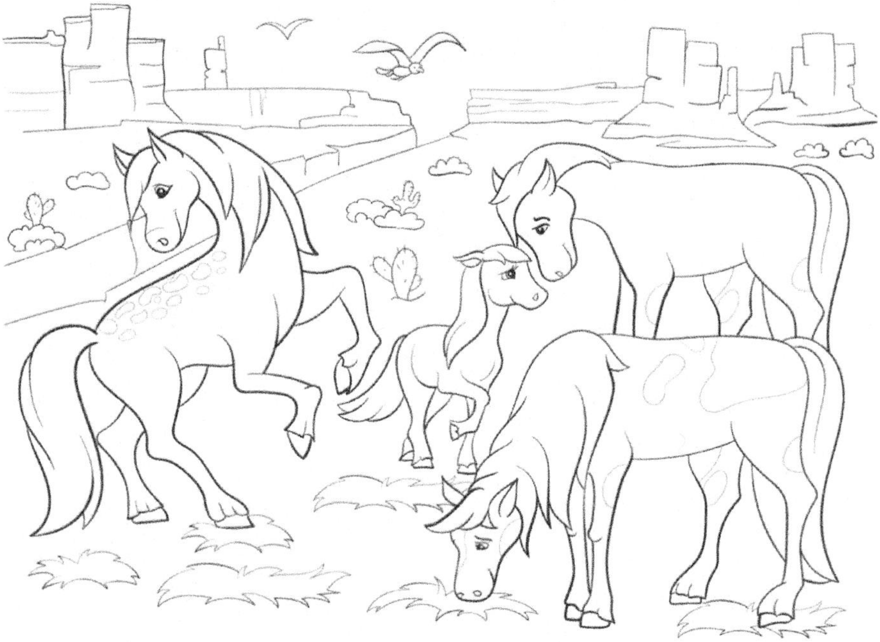

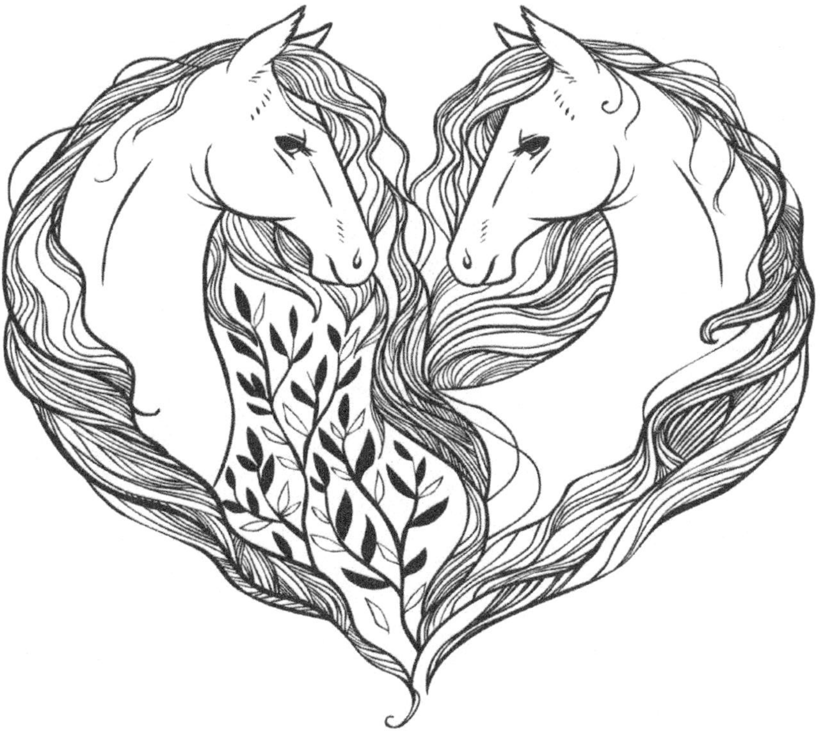

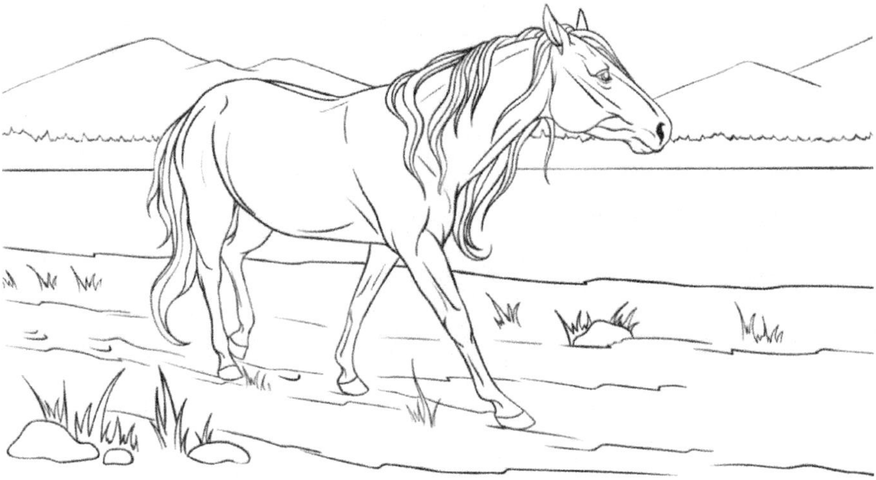

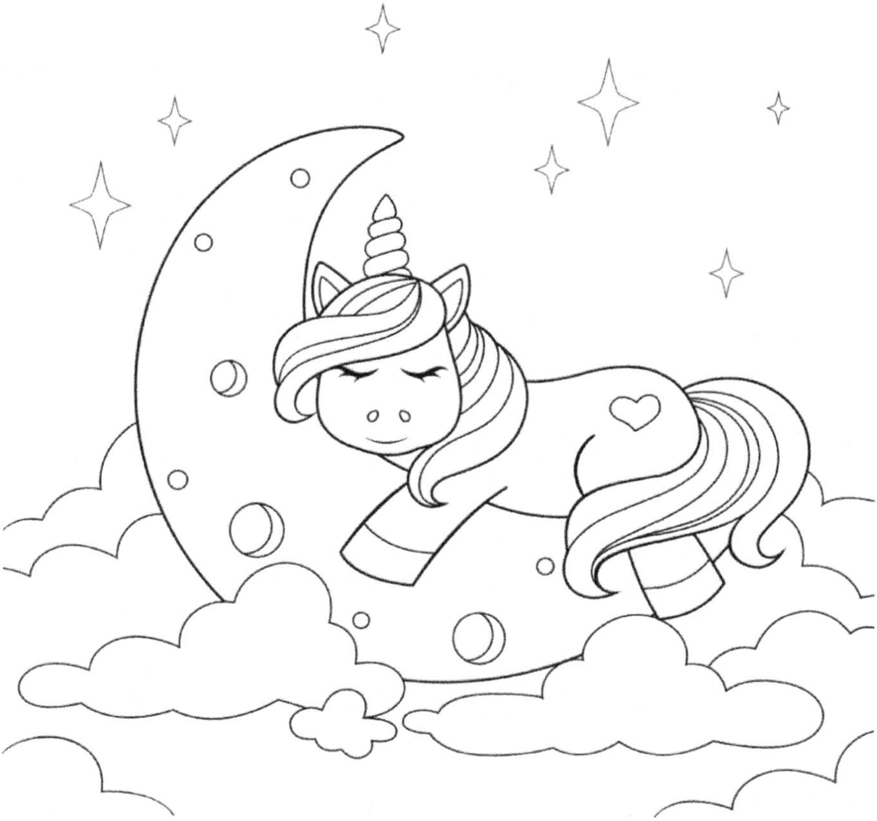

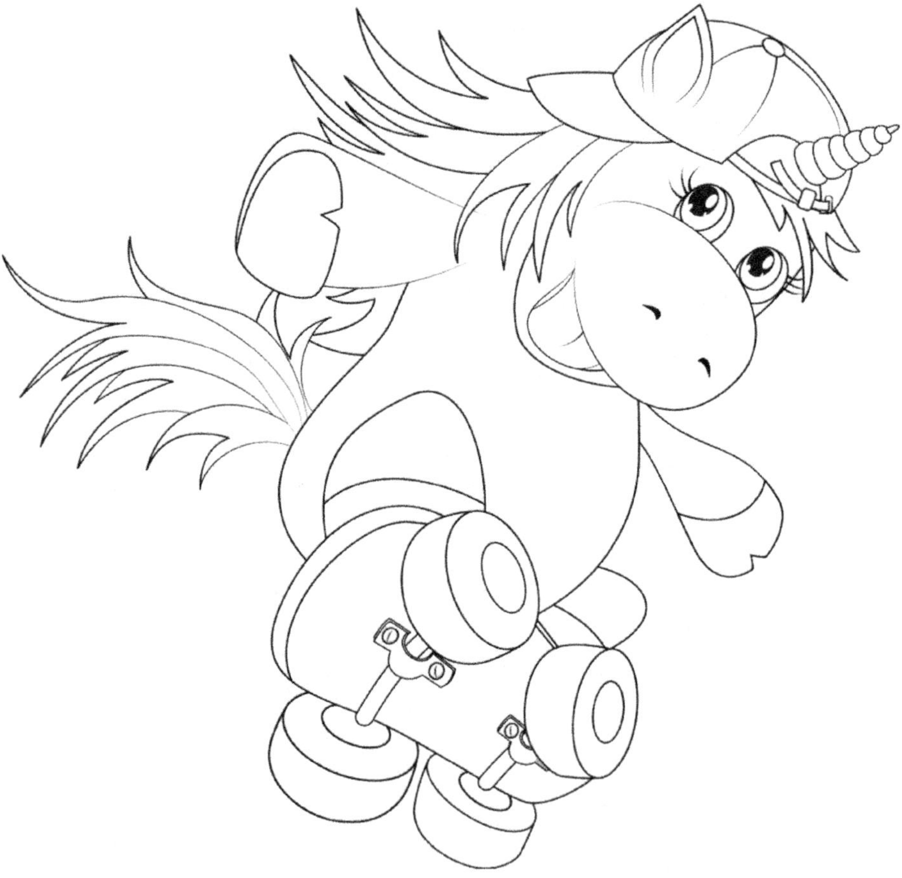

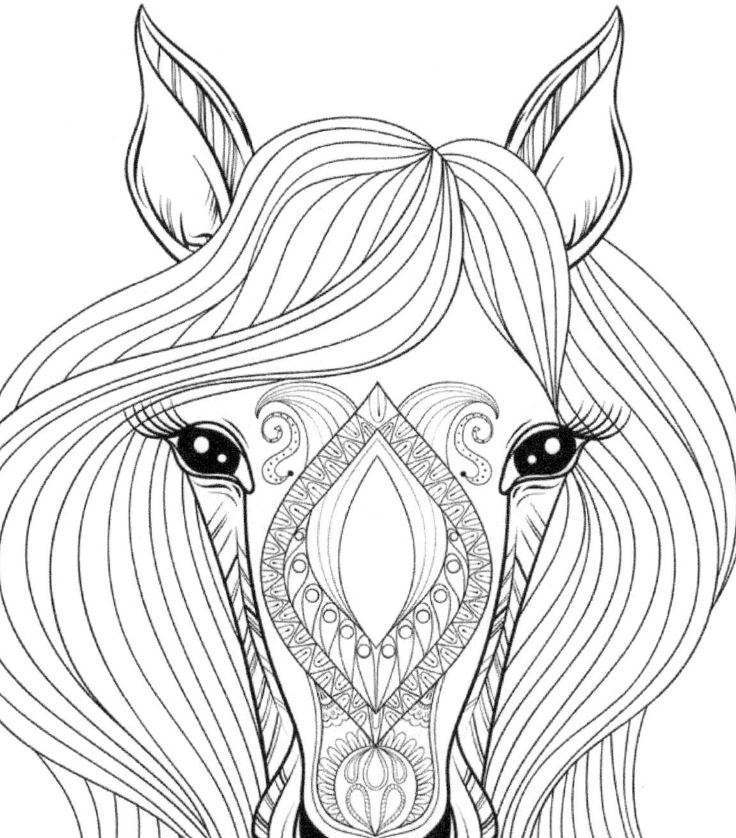

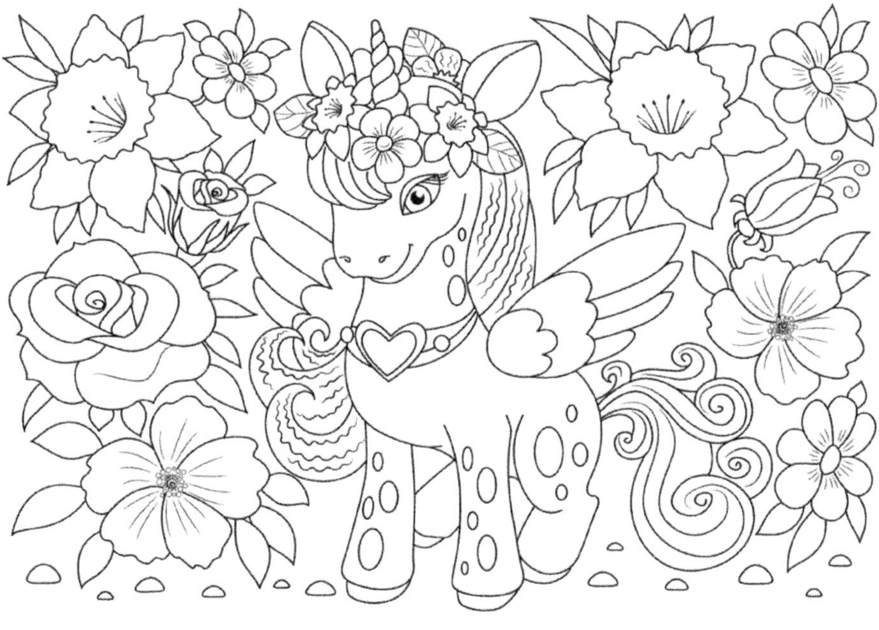

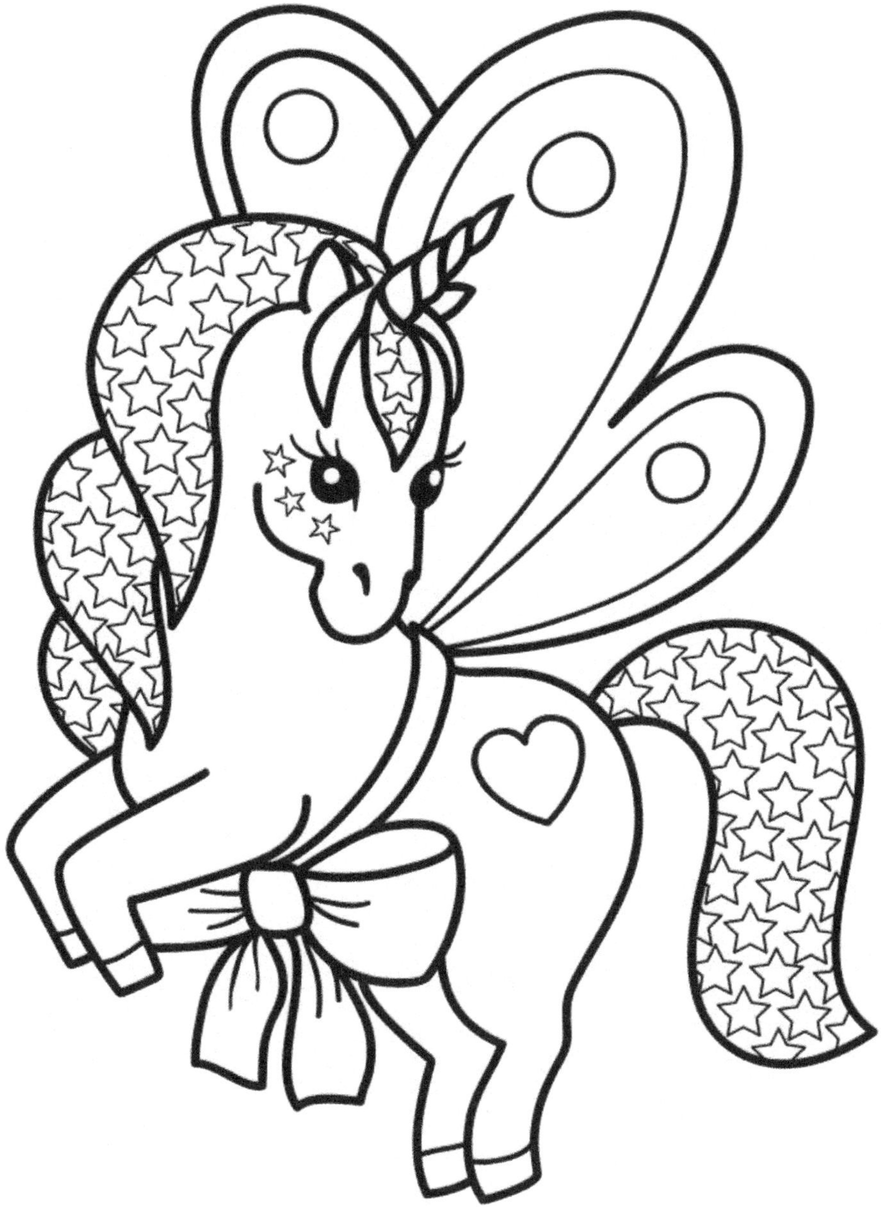

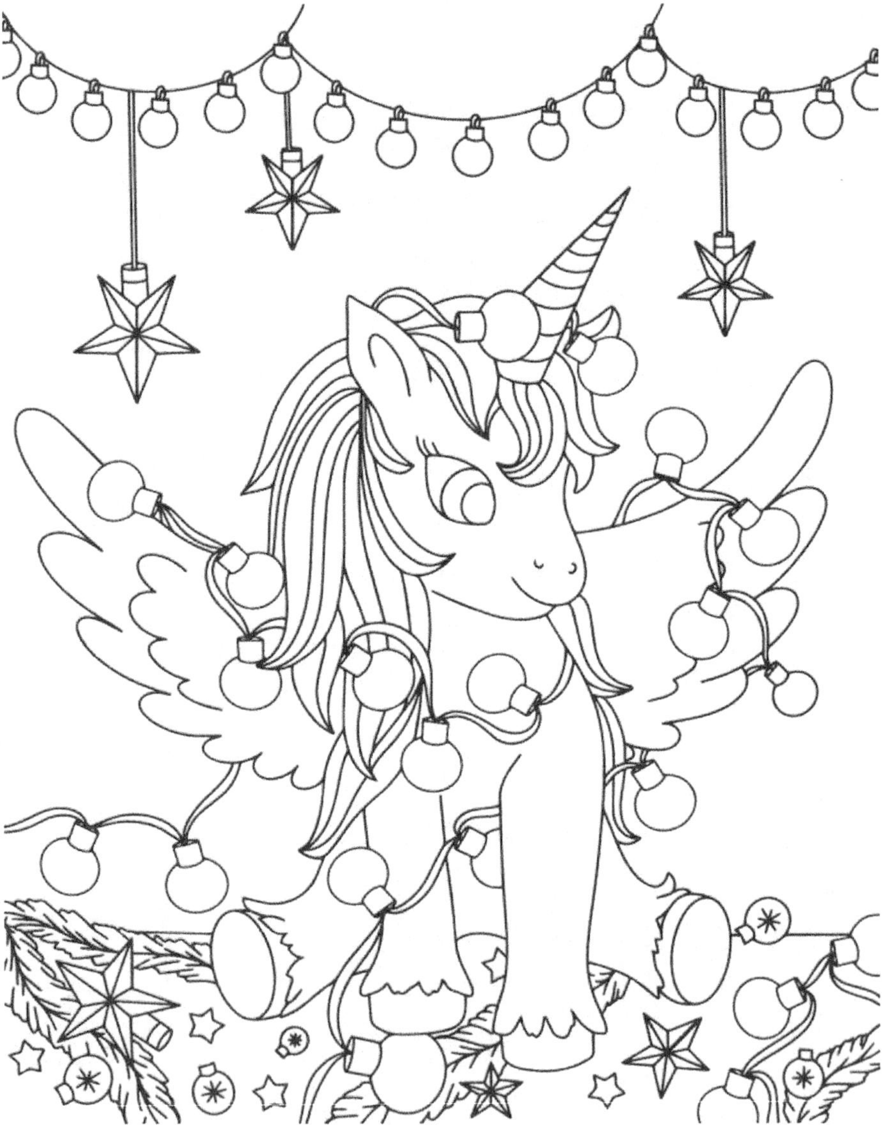

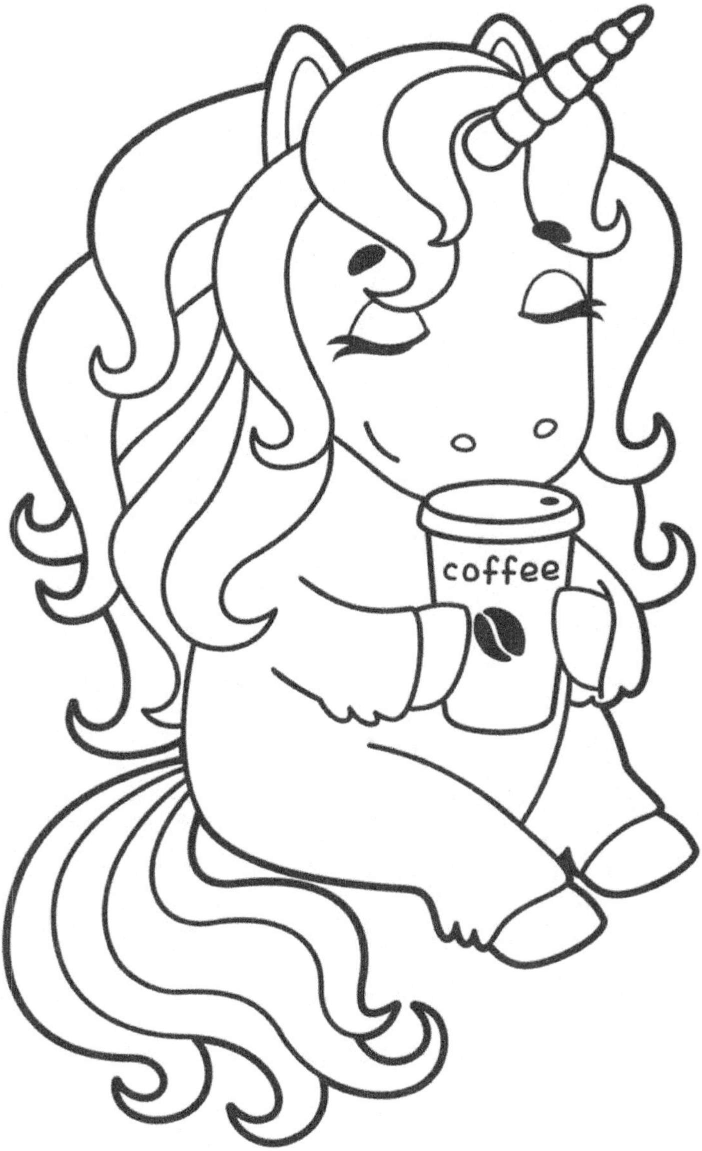
coffee

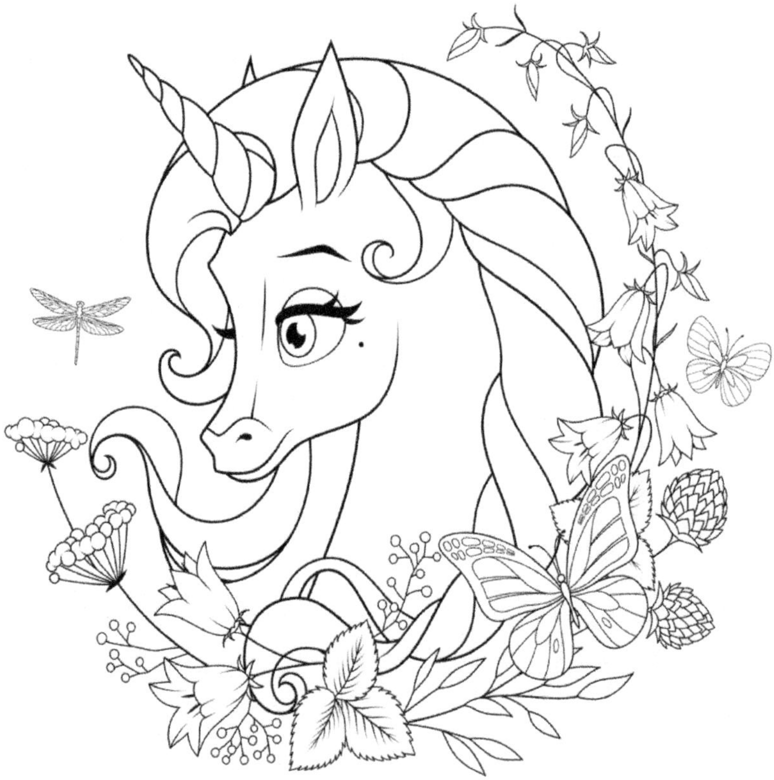

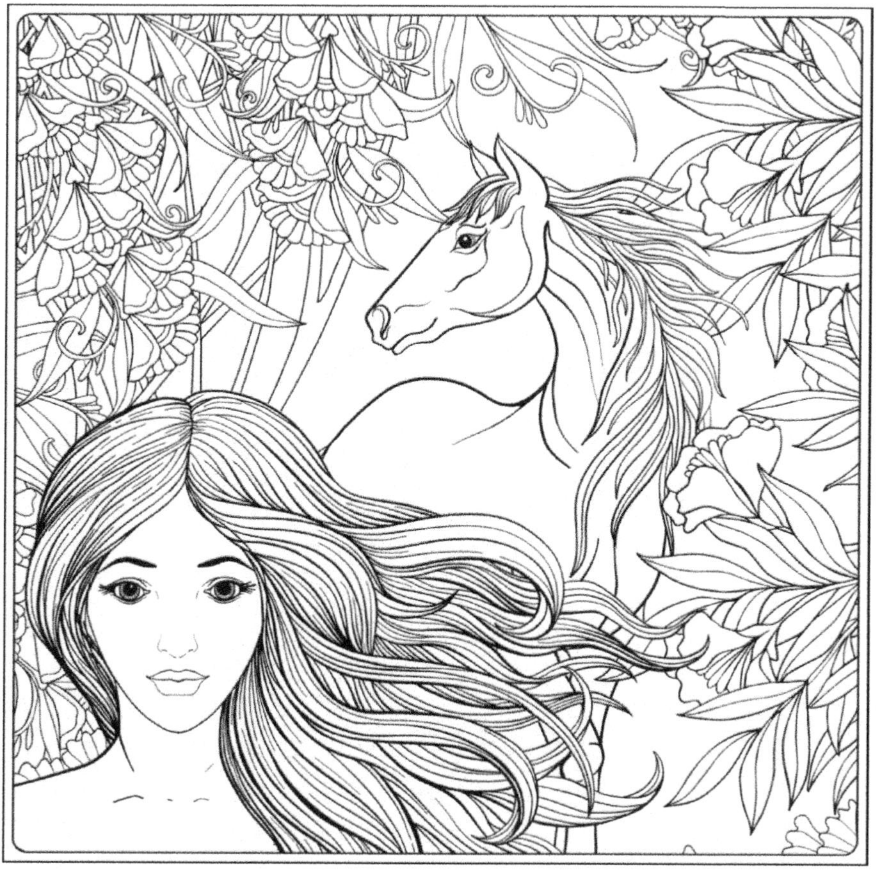

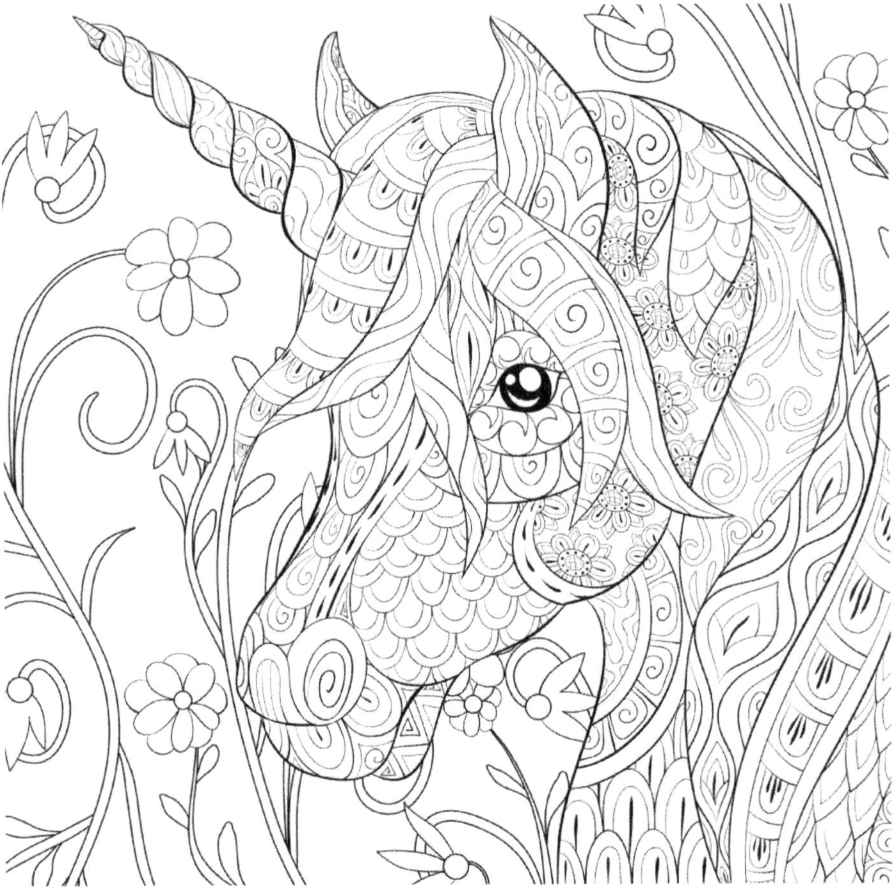

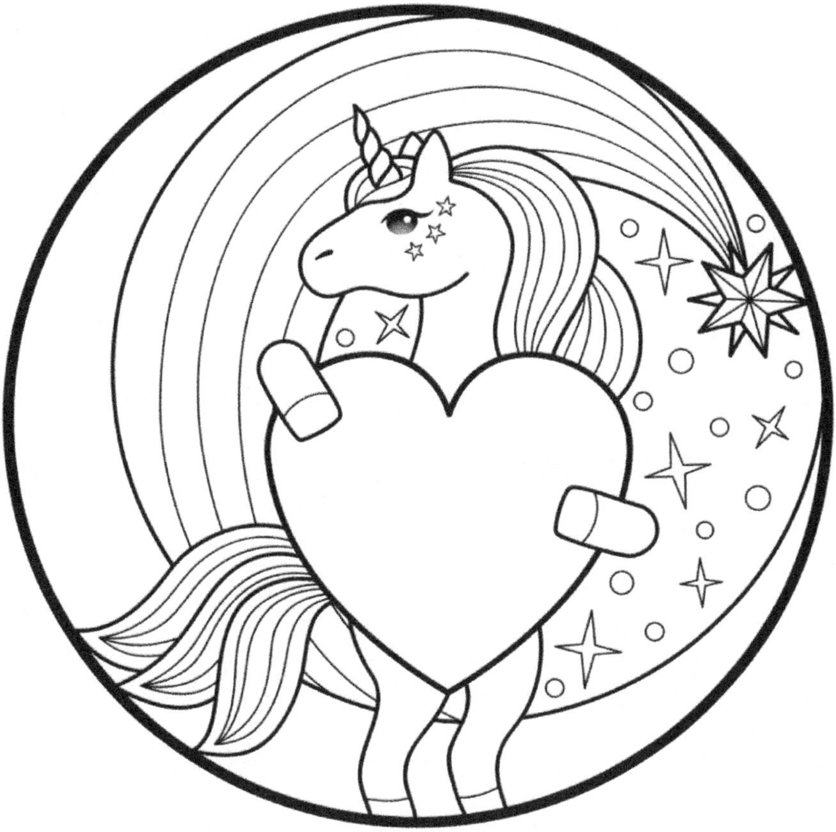

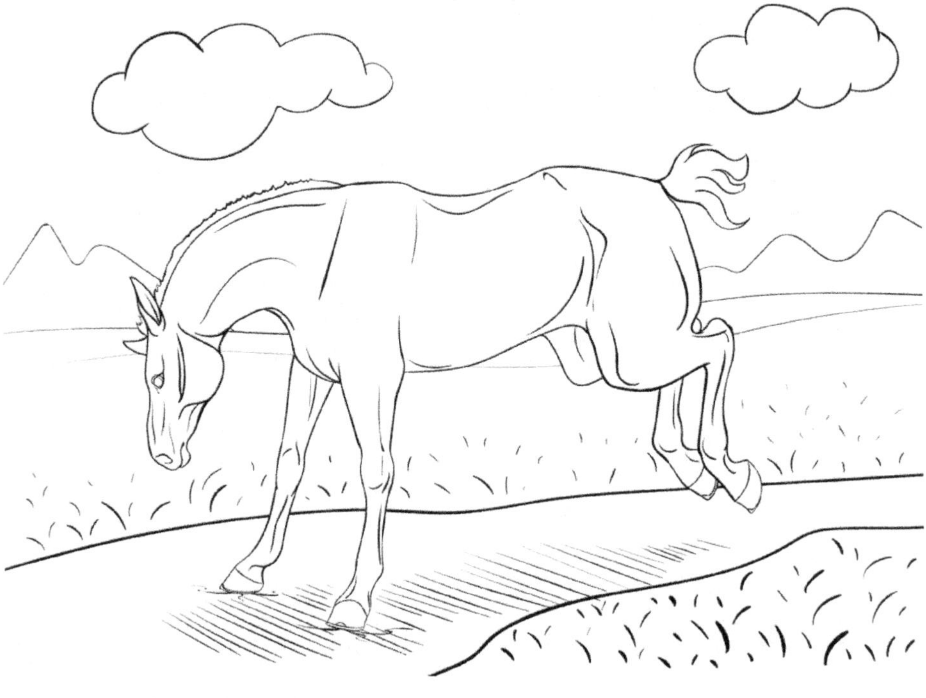

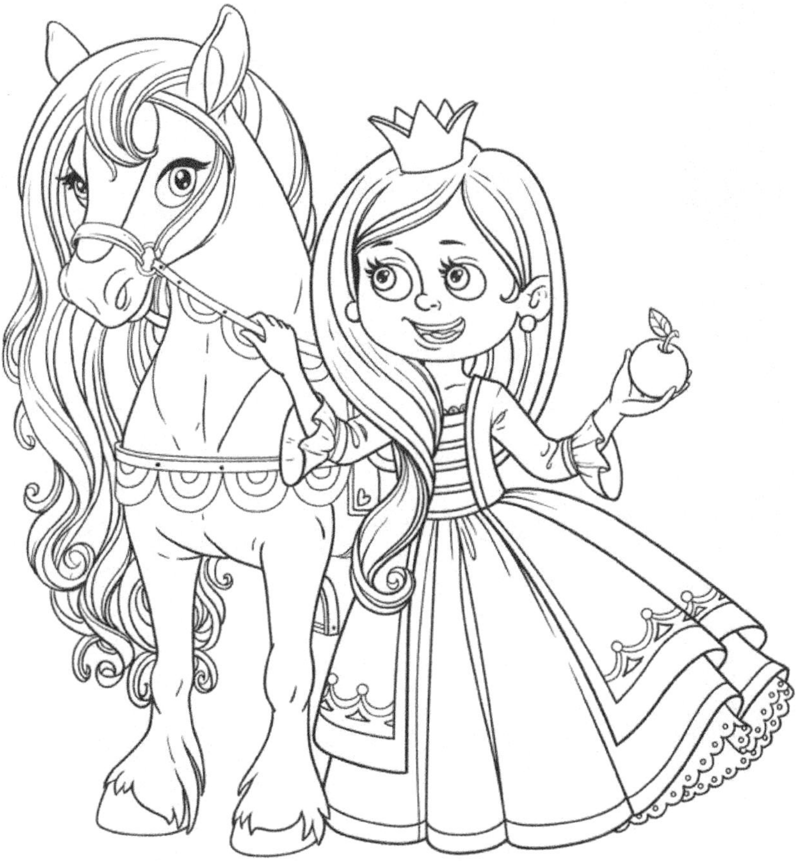

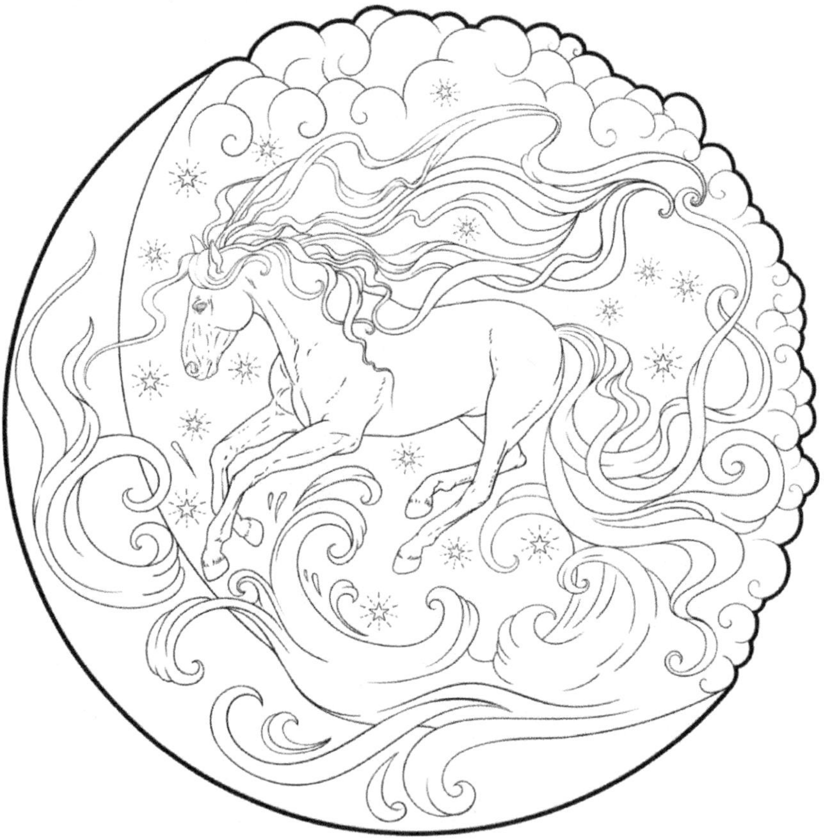

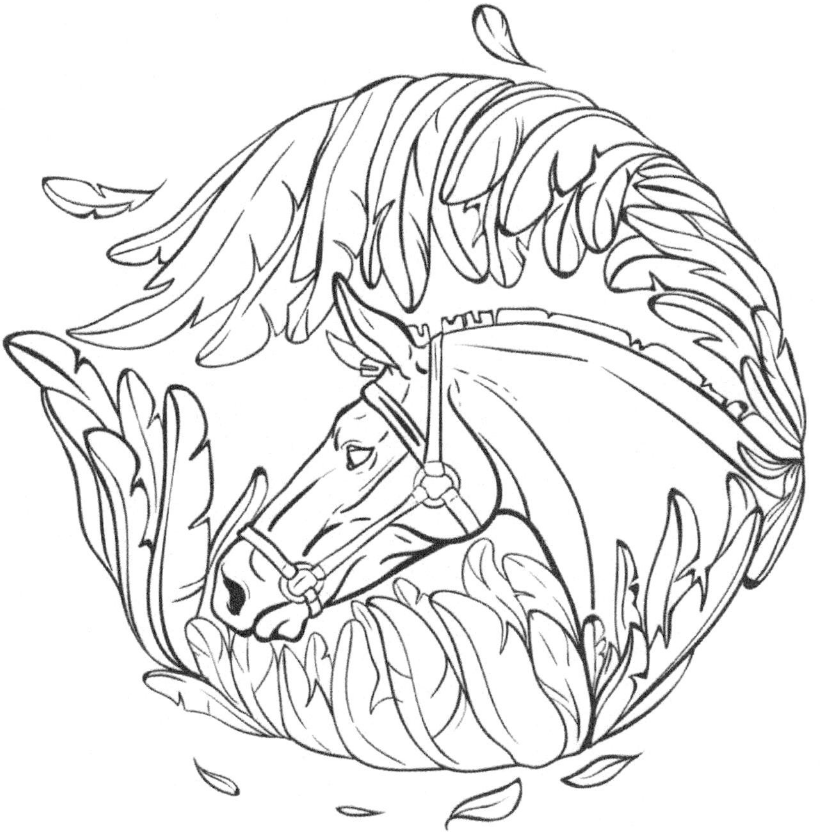

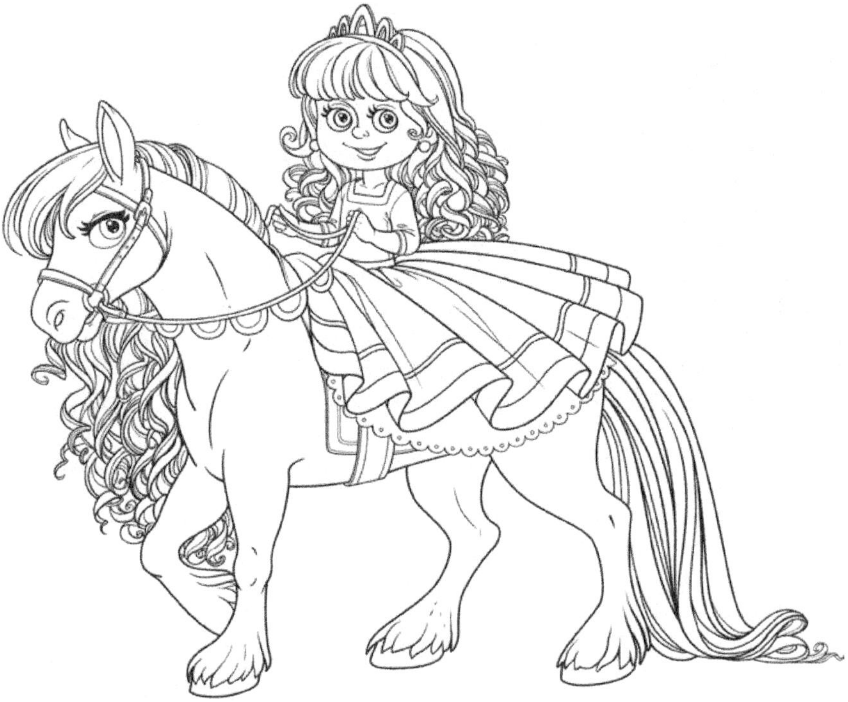

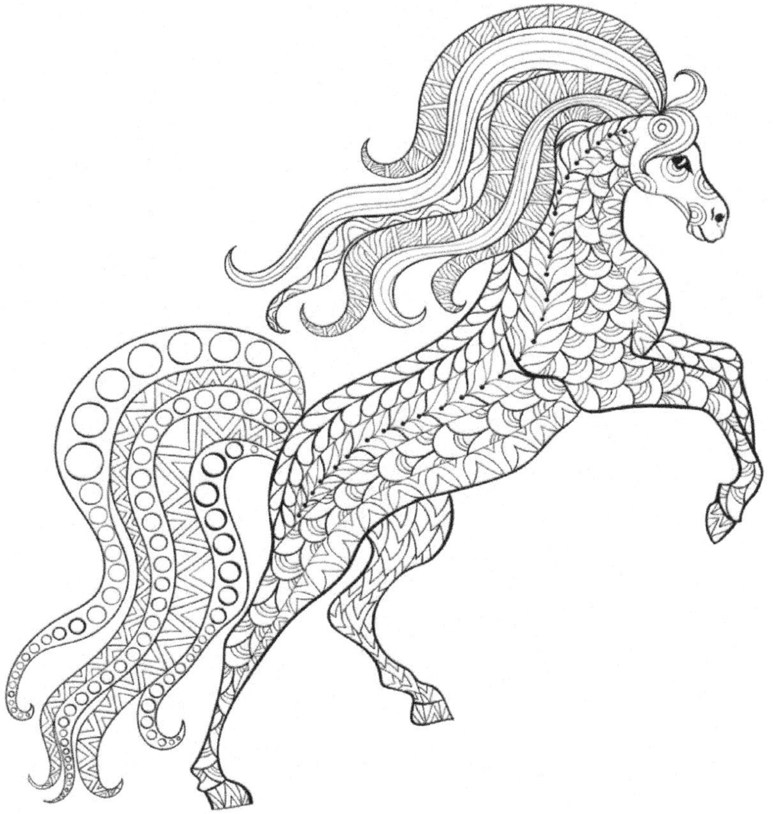

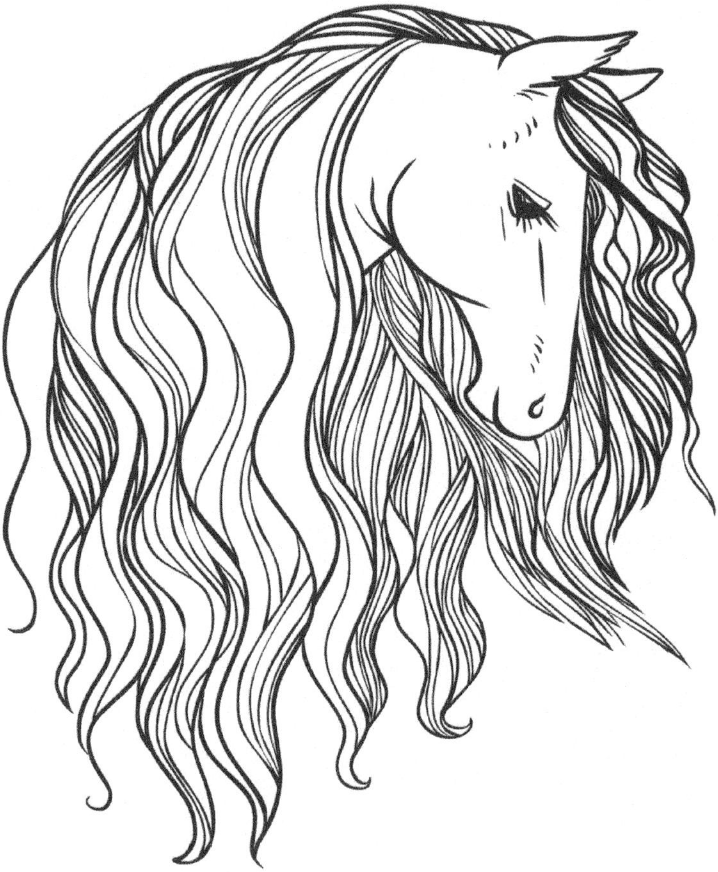

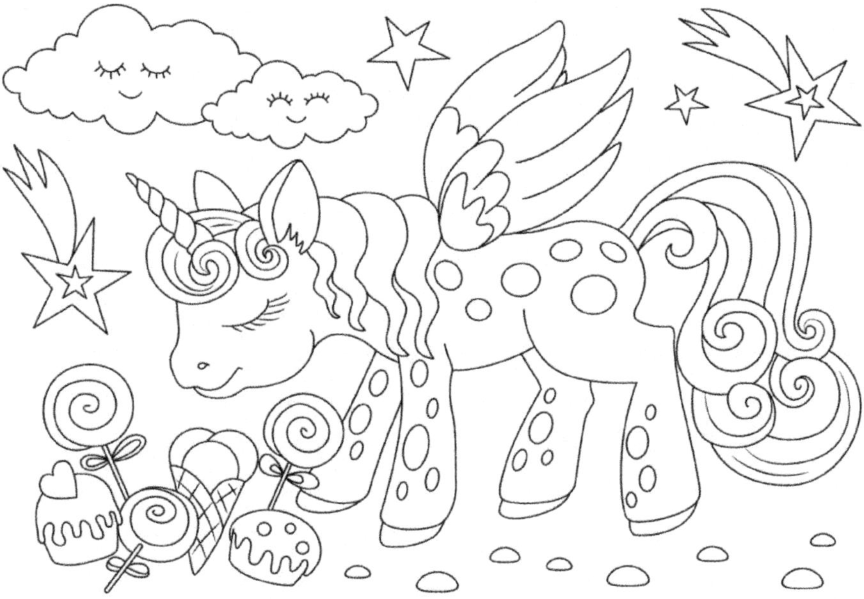

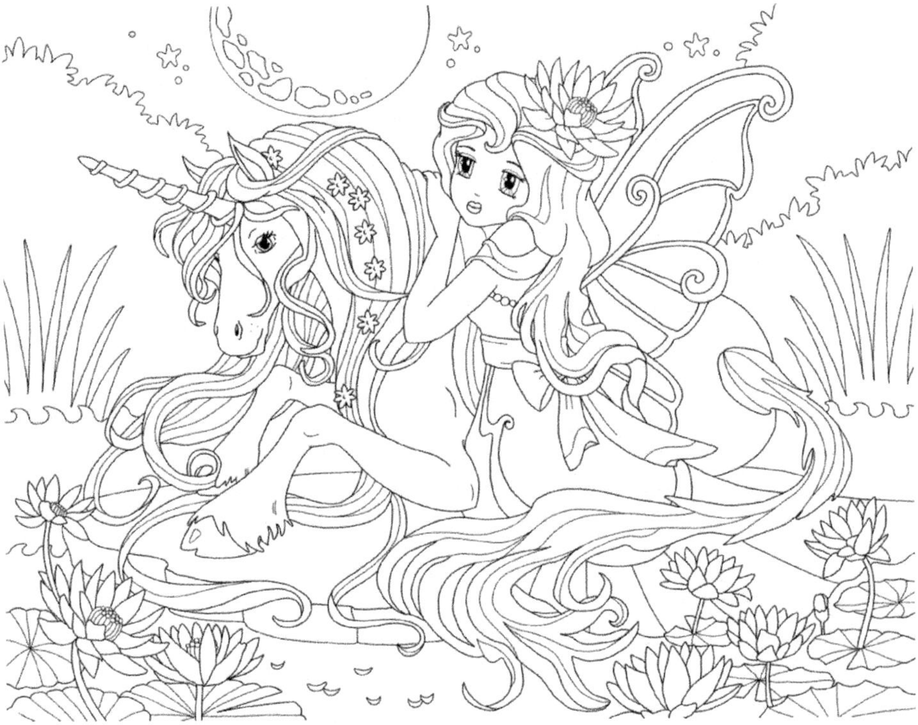

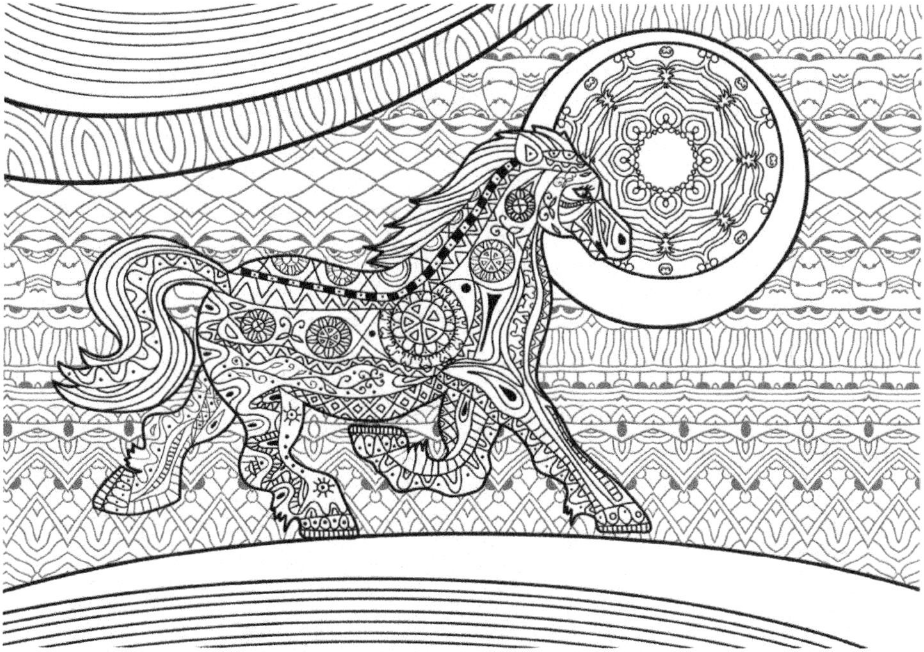

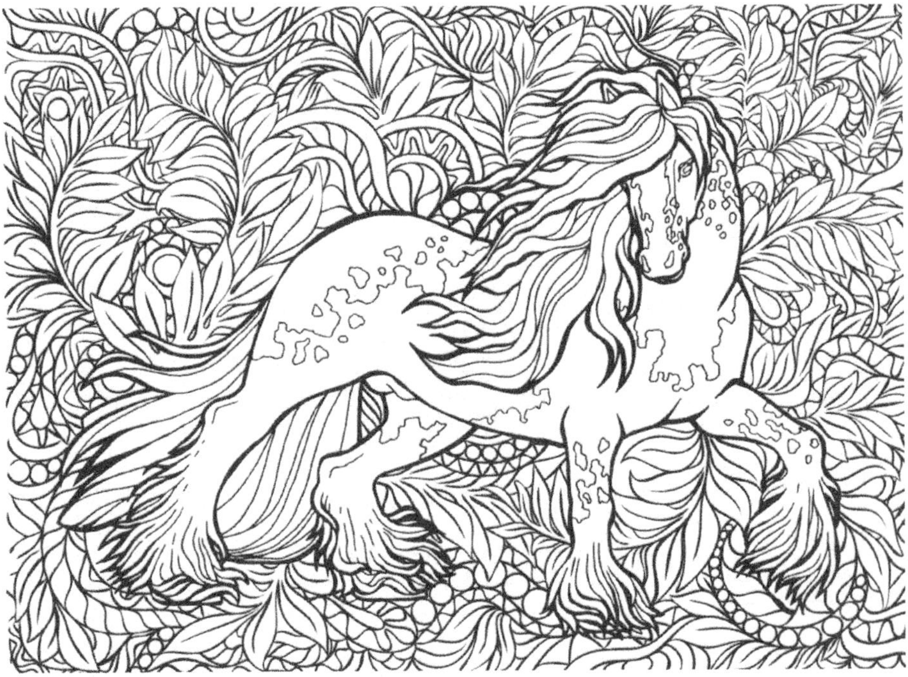

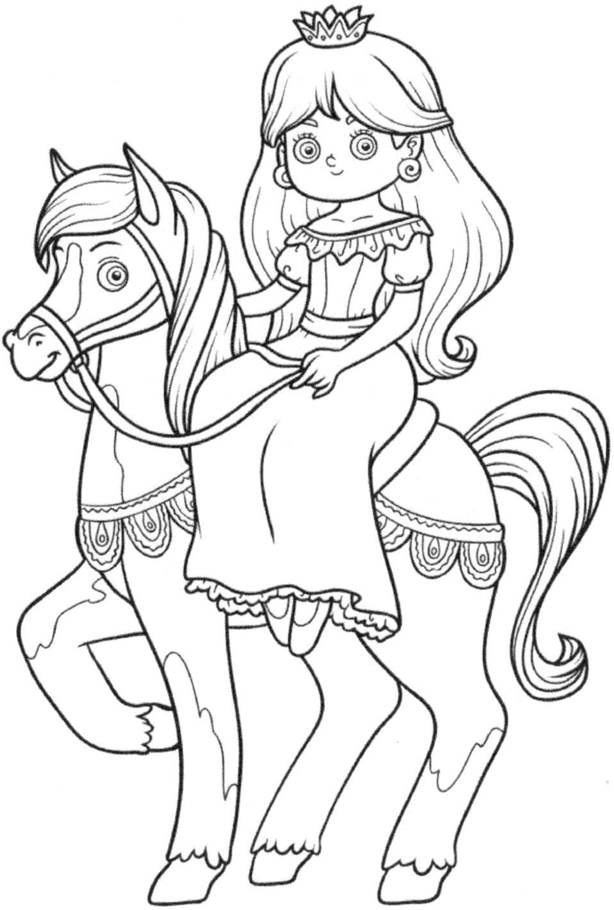

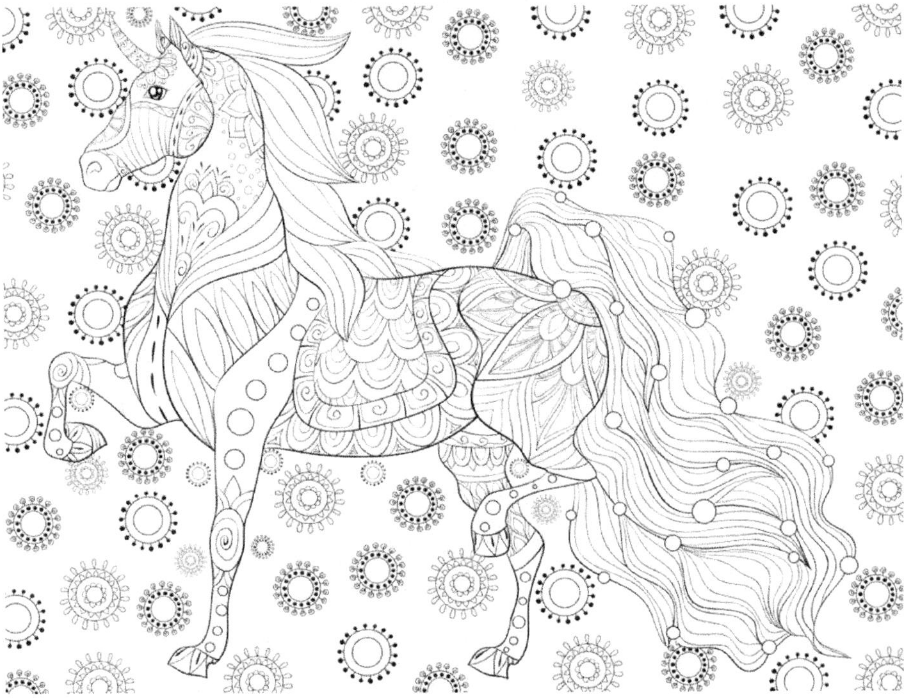

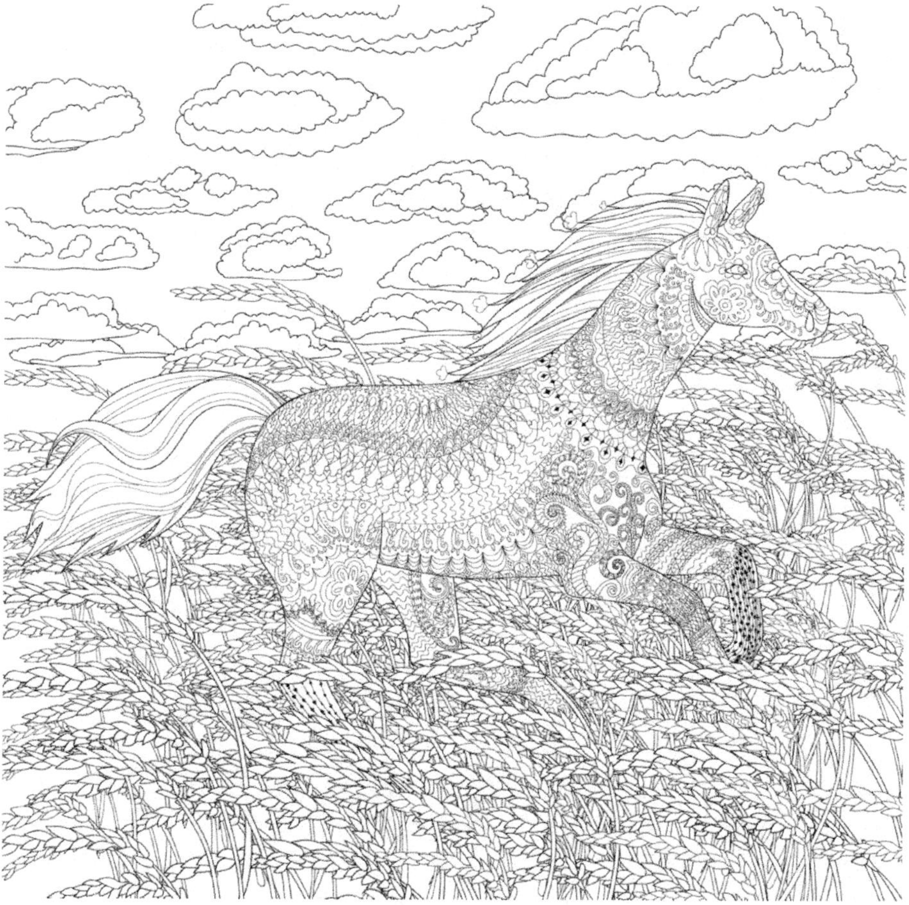

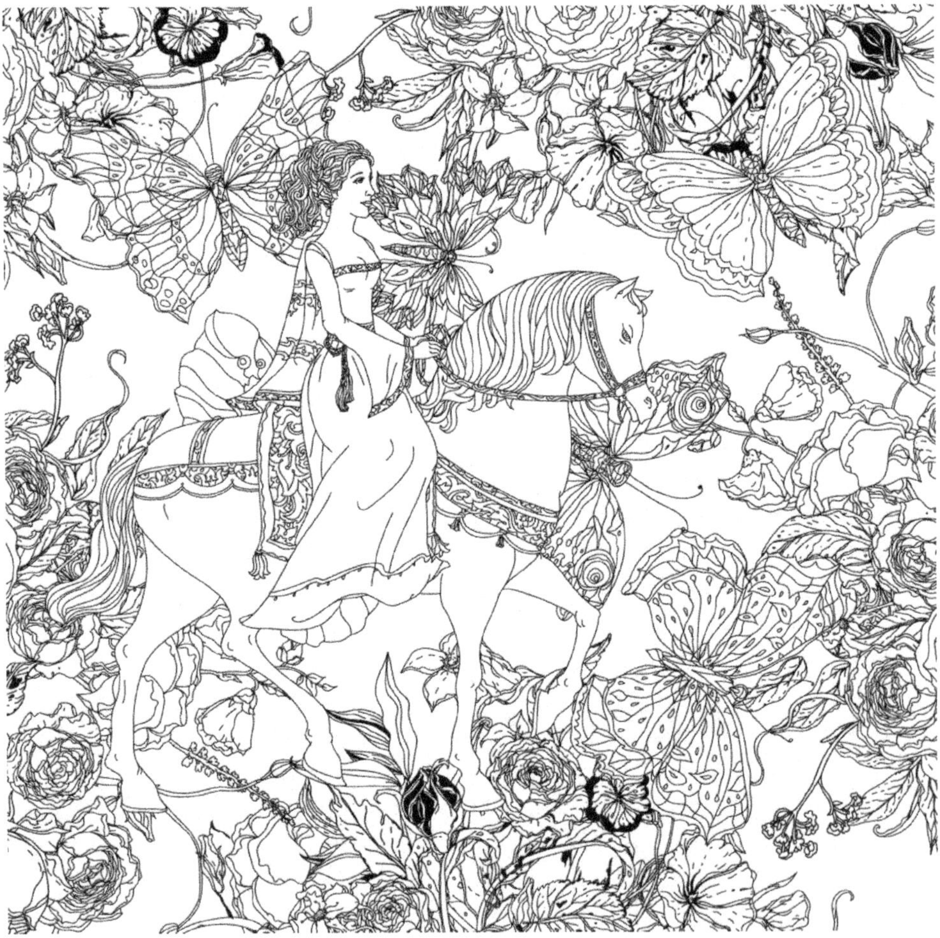

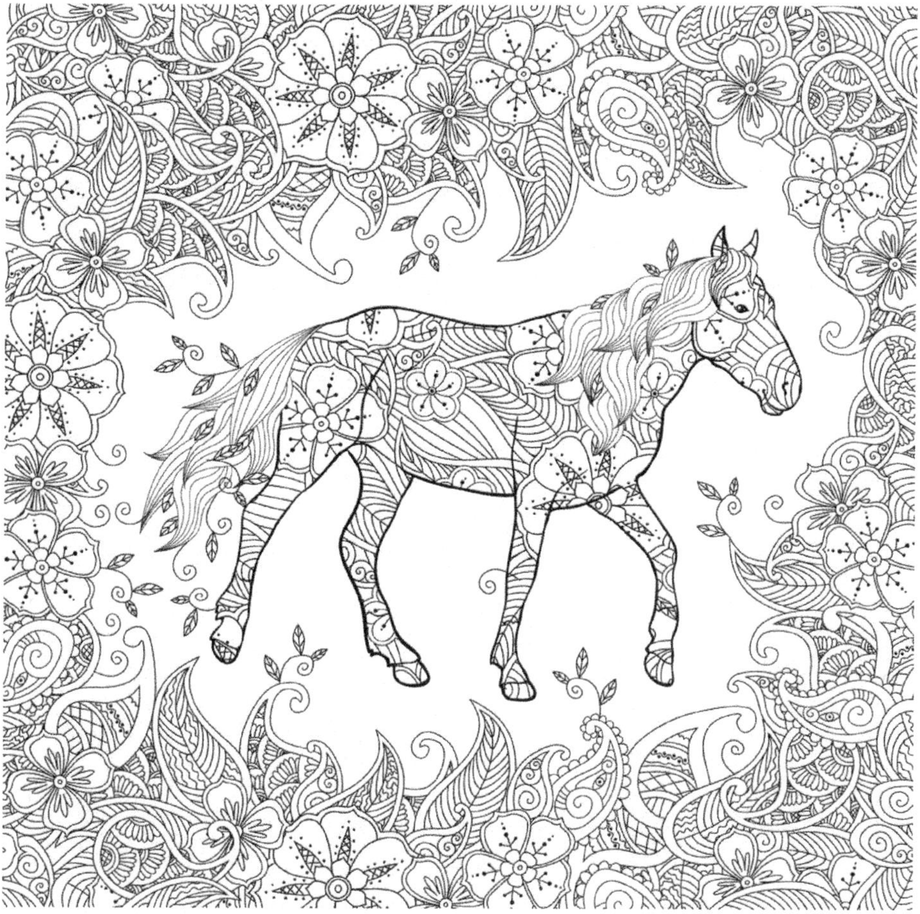

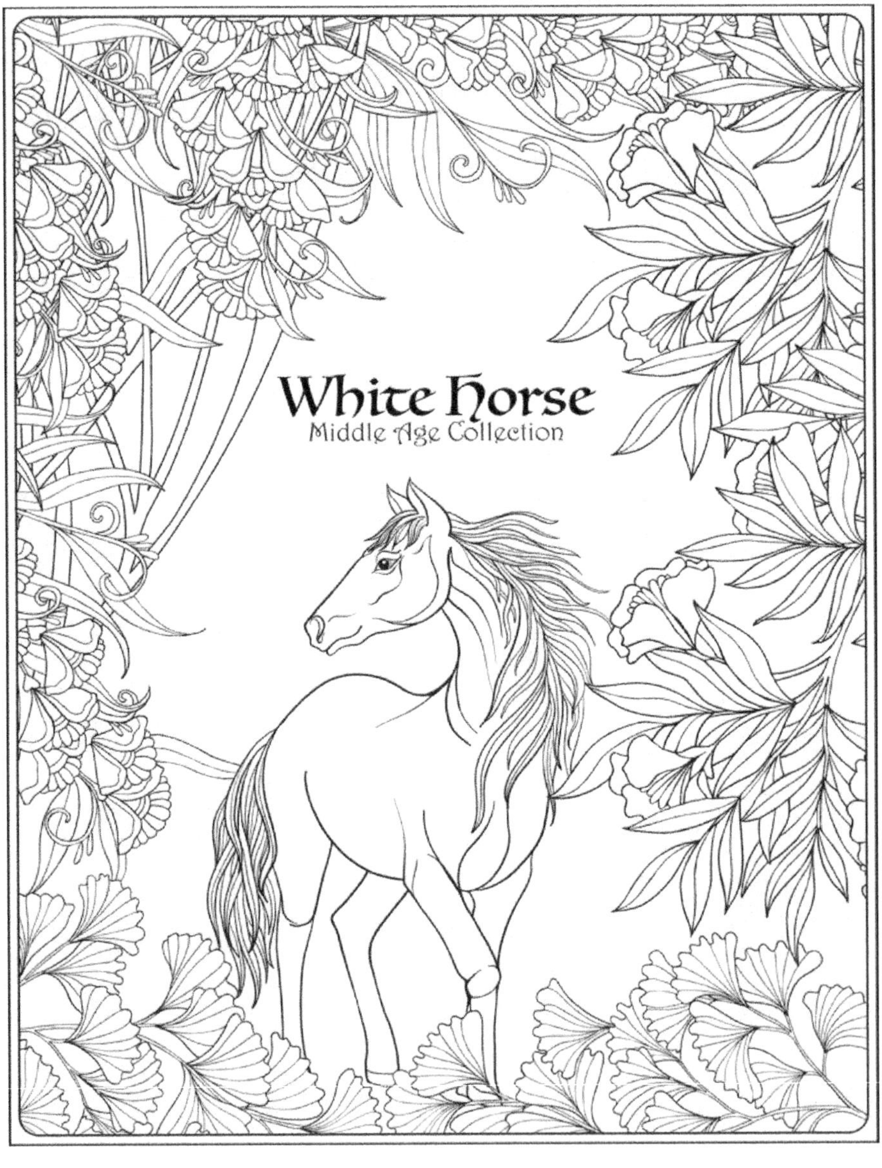
White Horse
Middle Age Collection

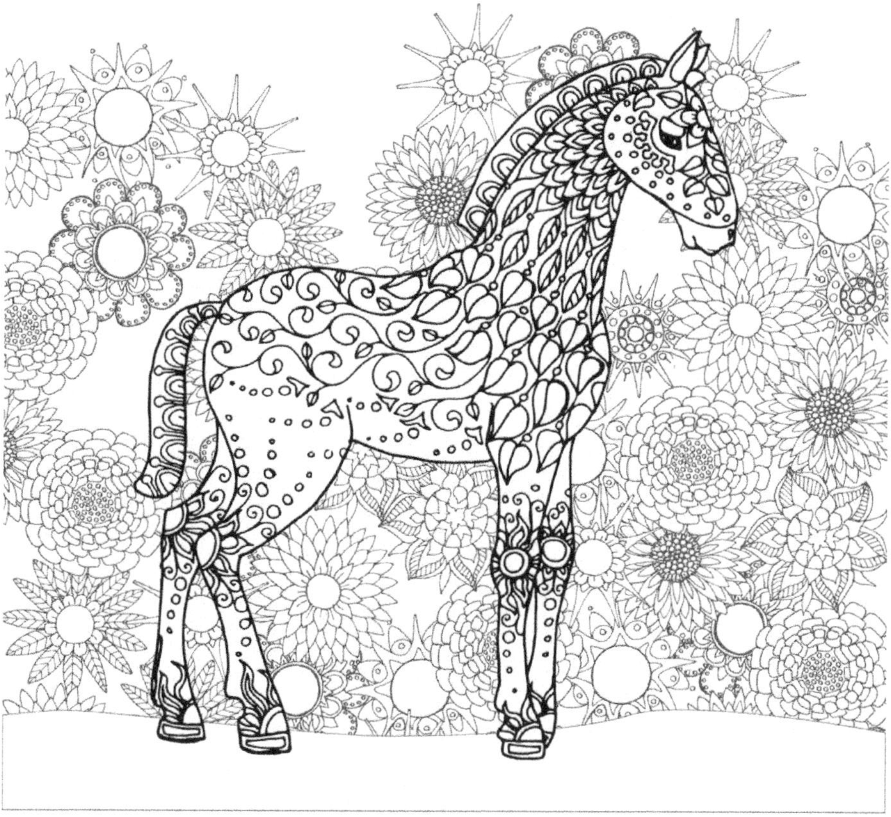

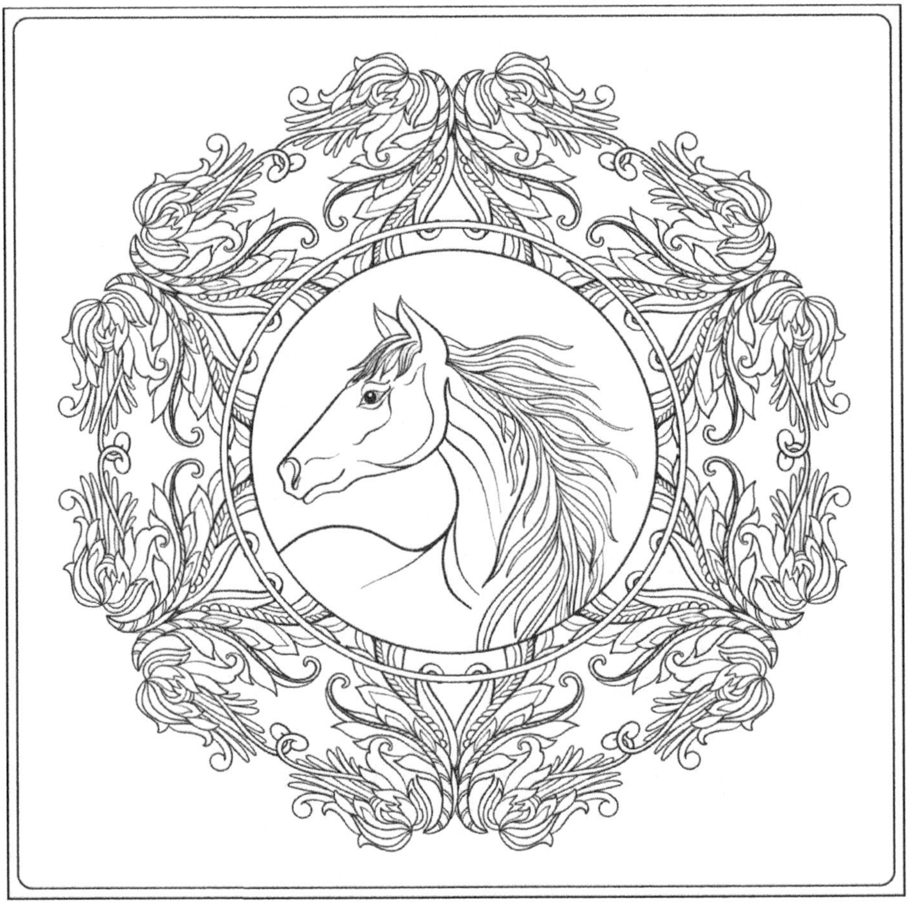

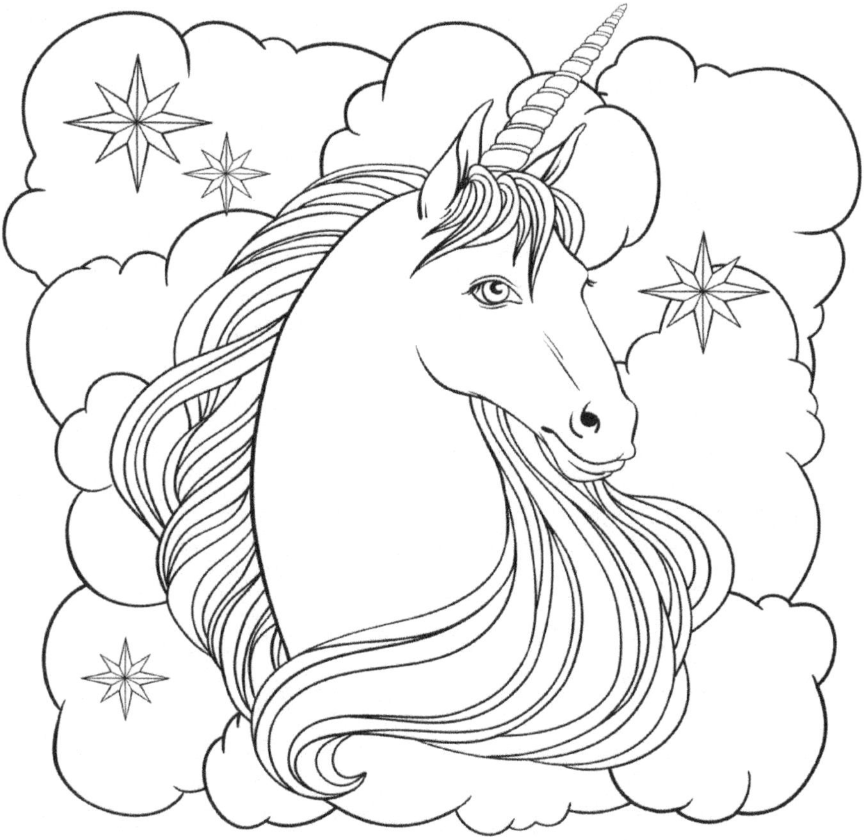

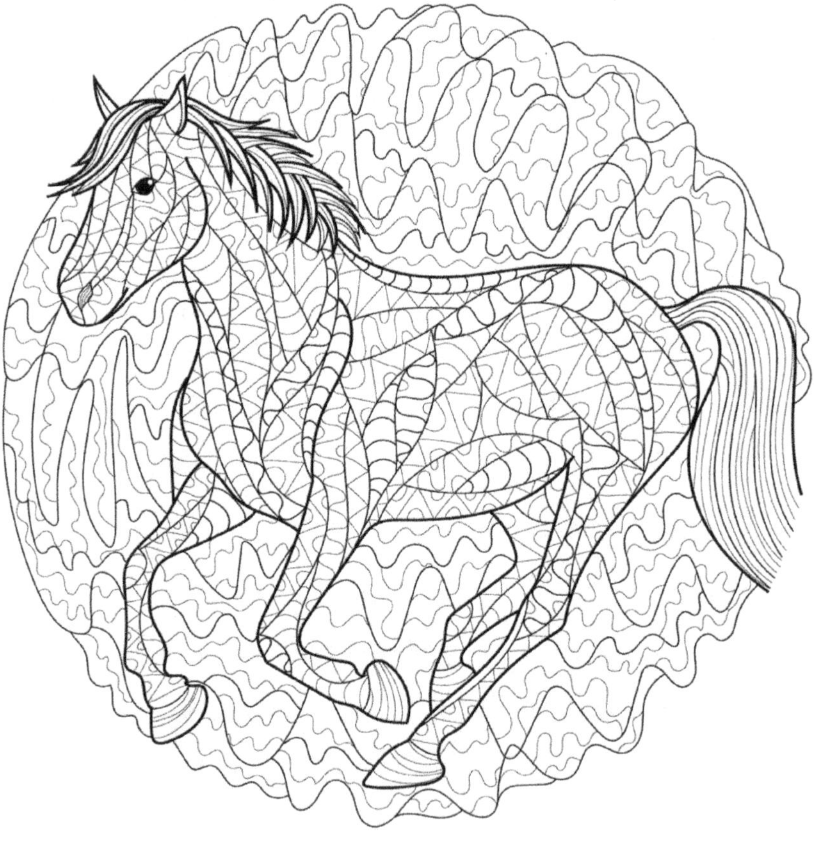

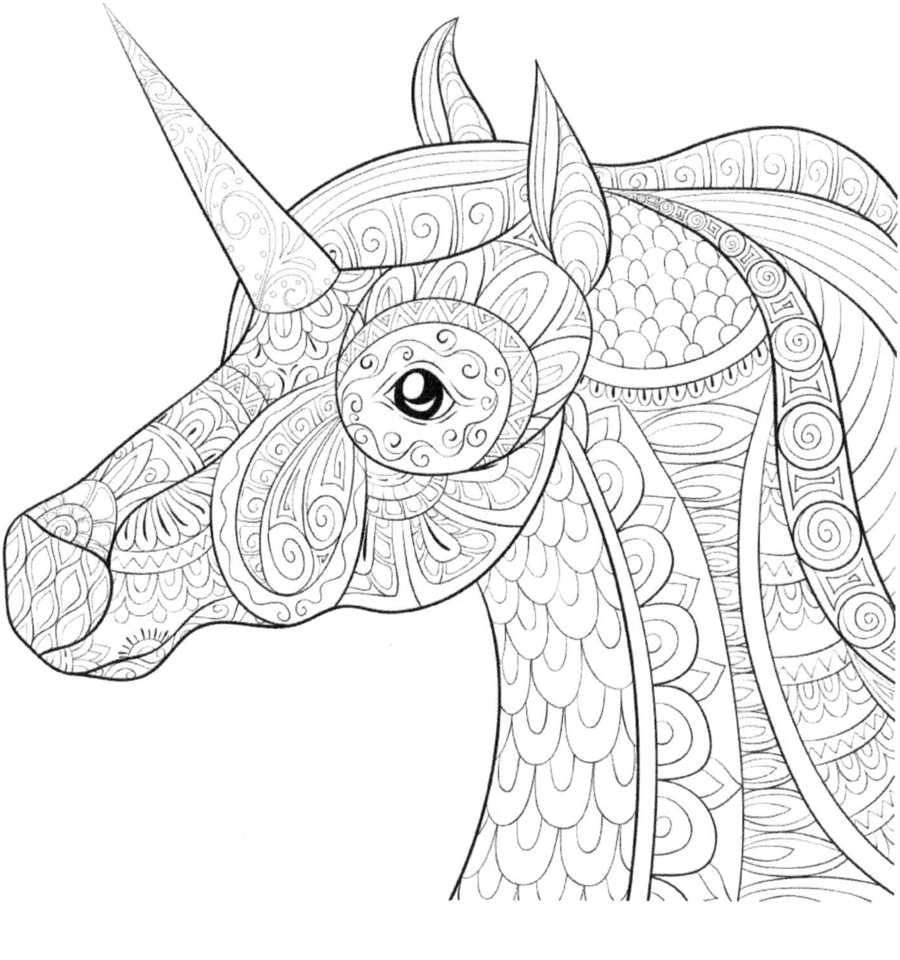

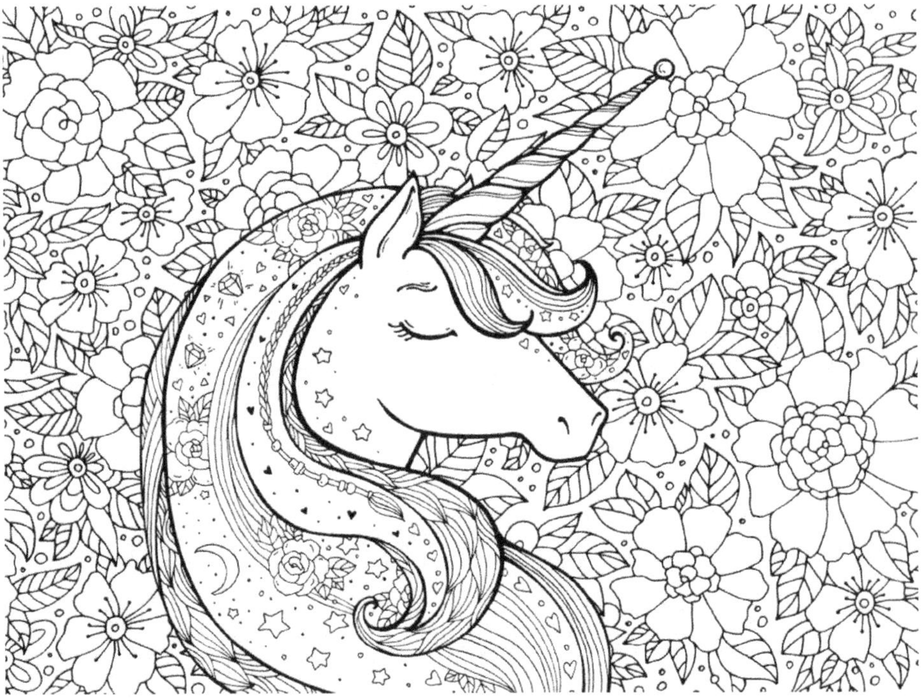

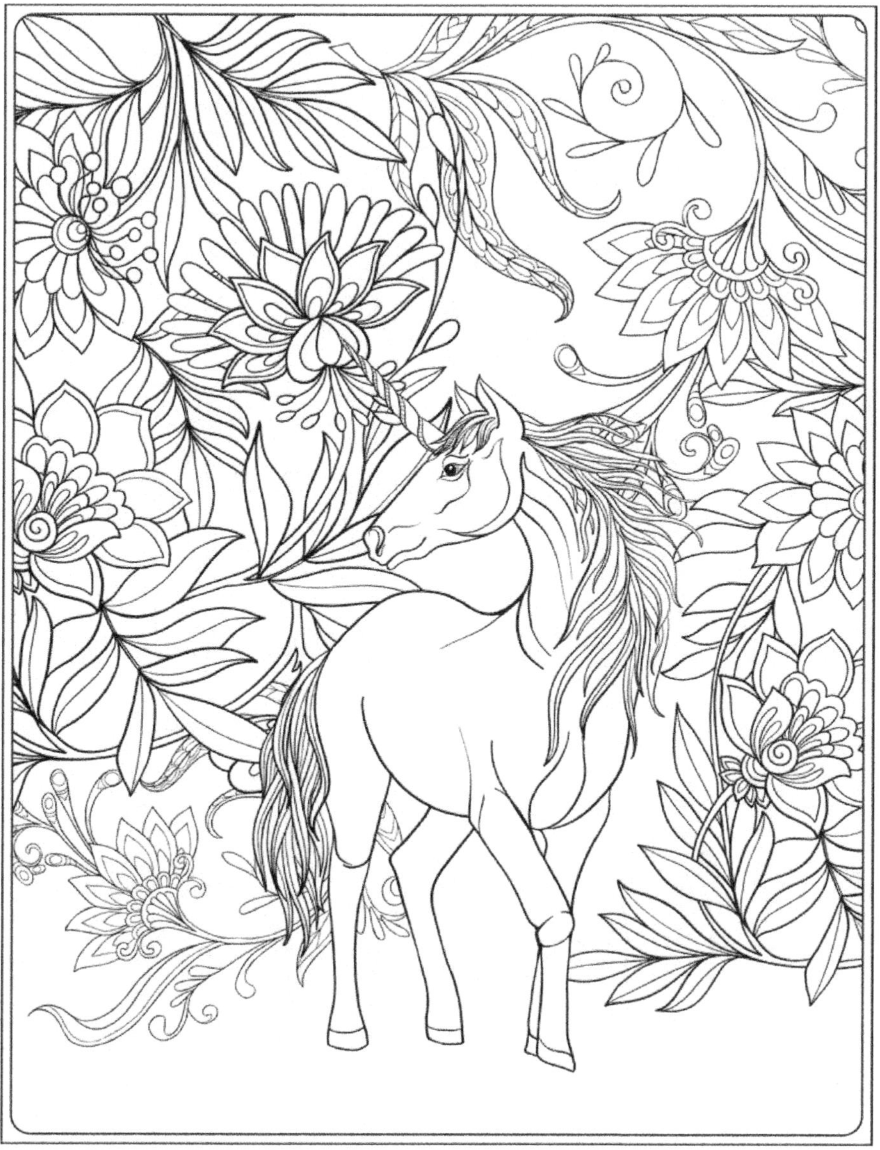

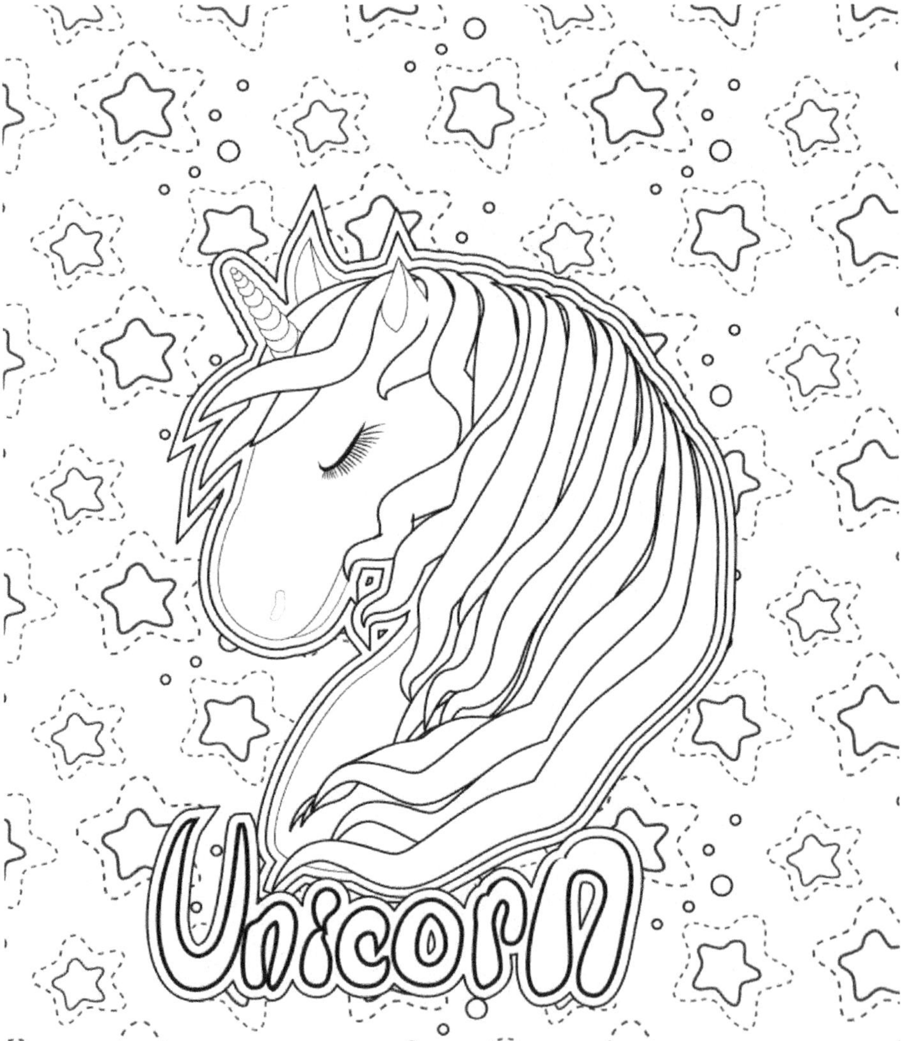
Unicorn

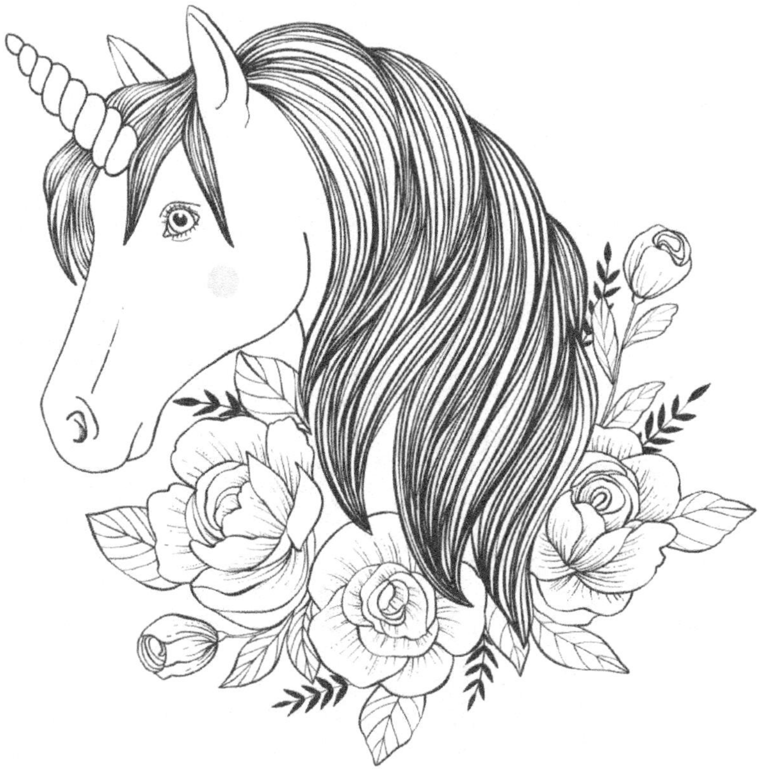

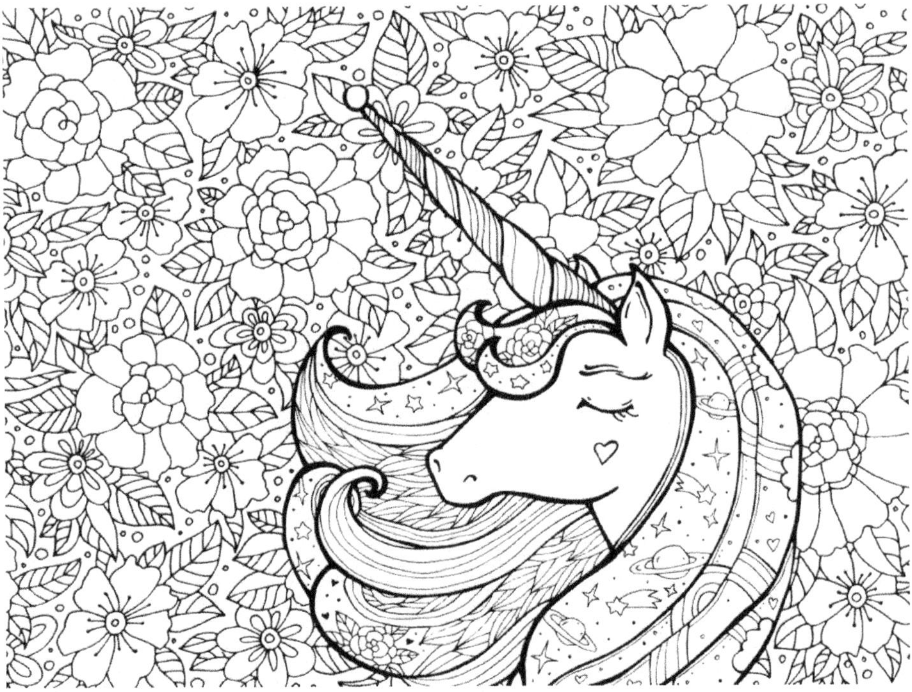

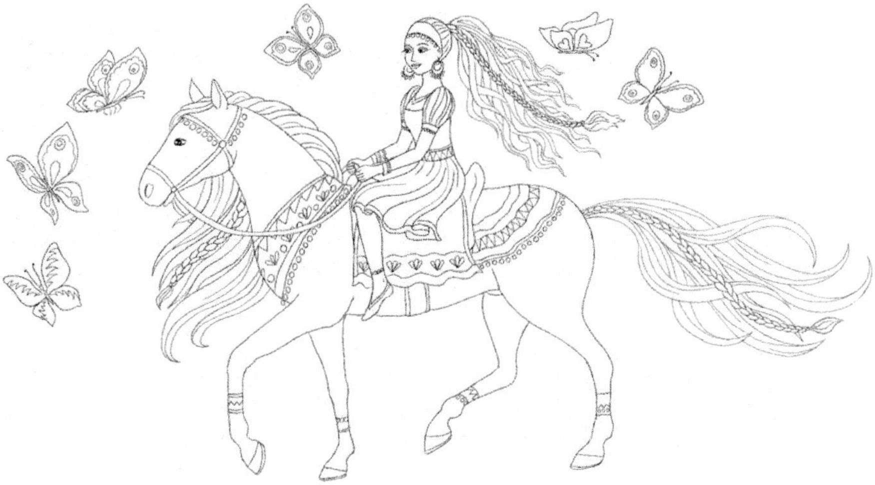

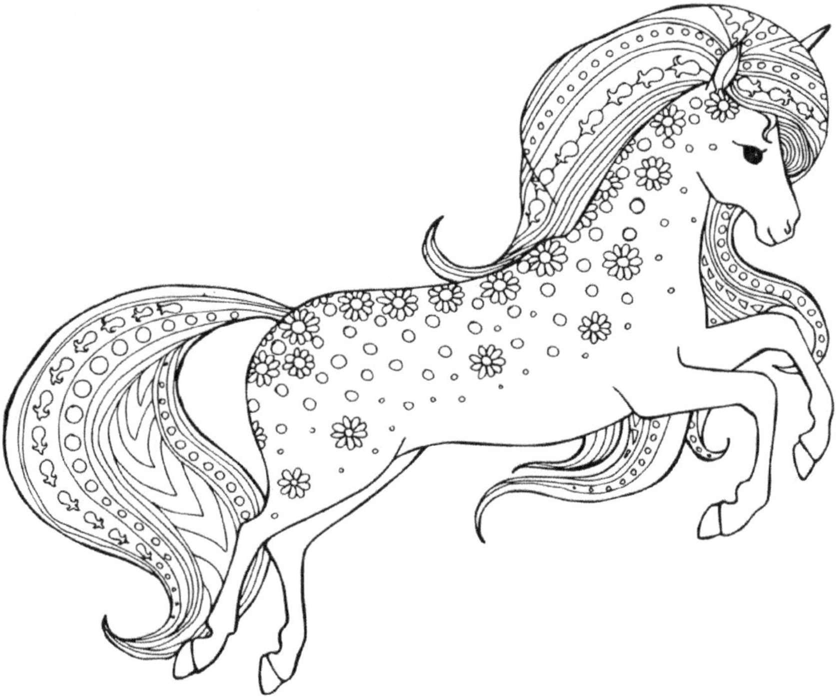

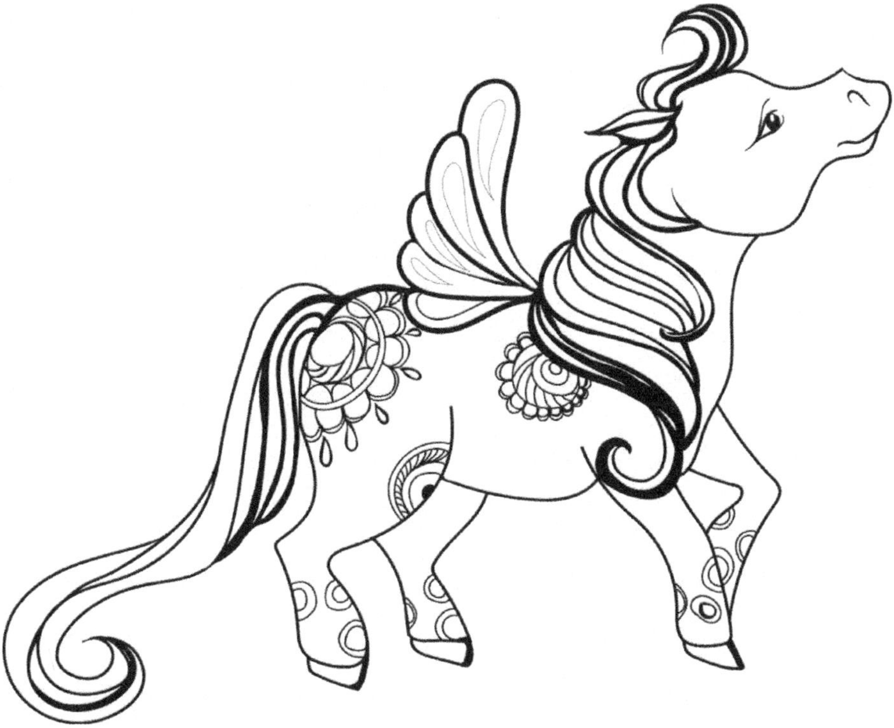

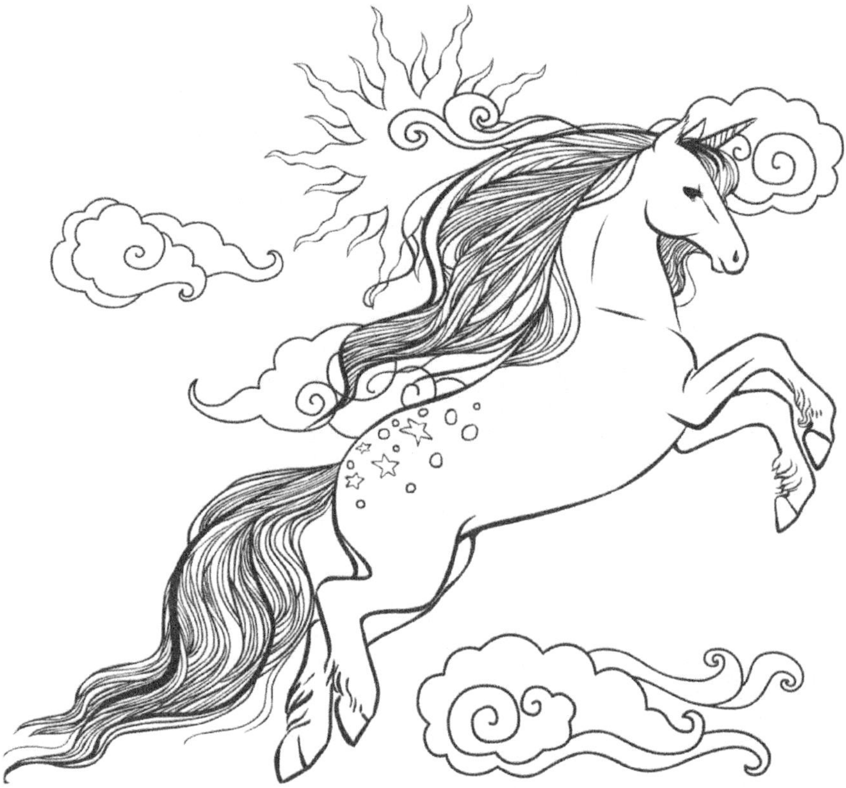

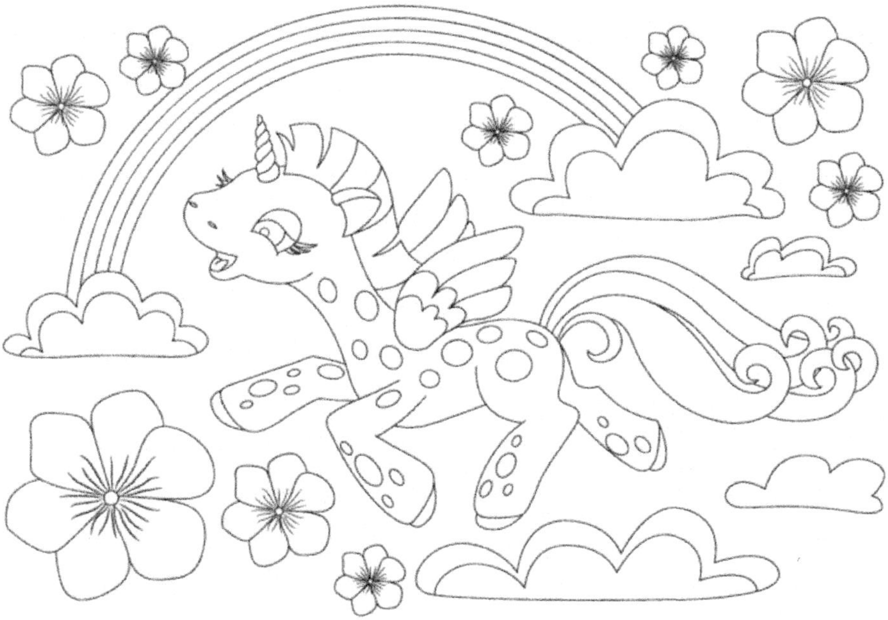

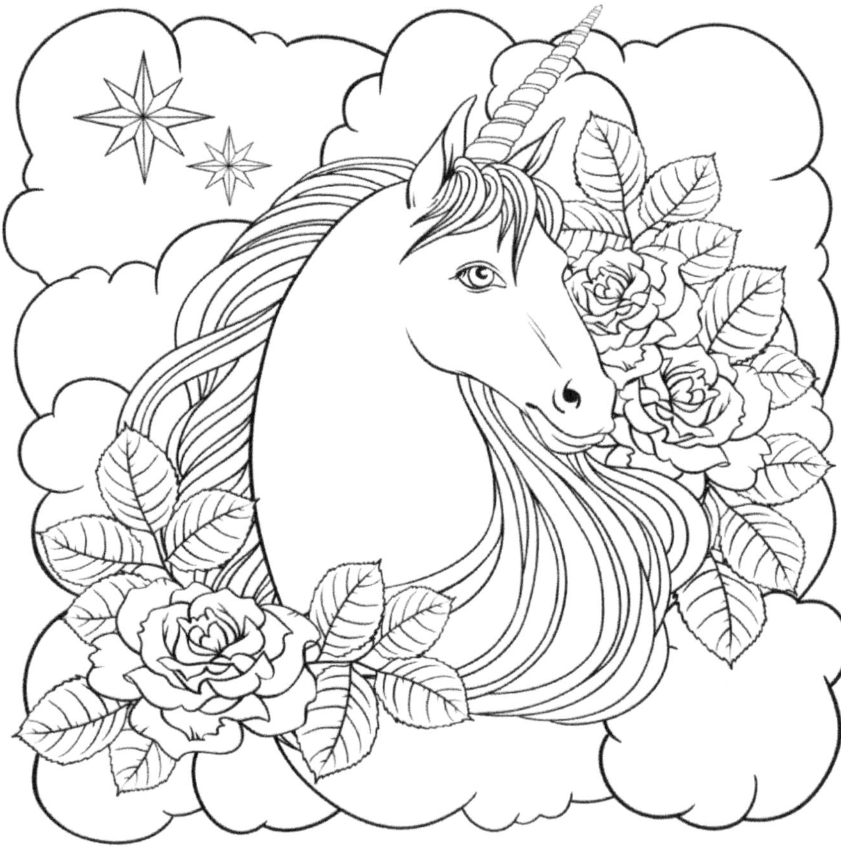

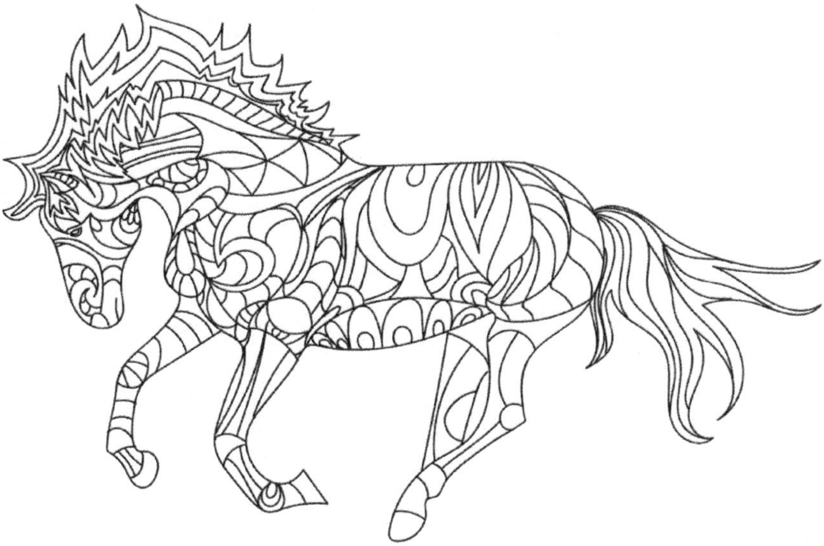

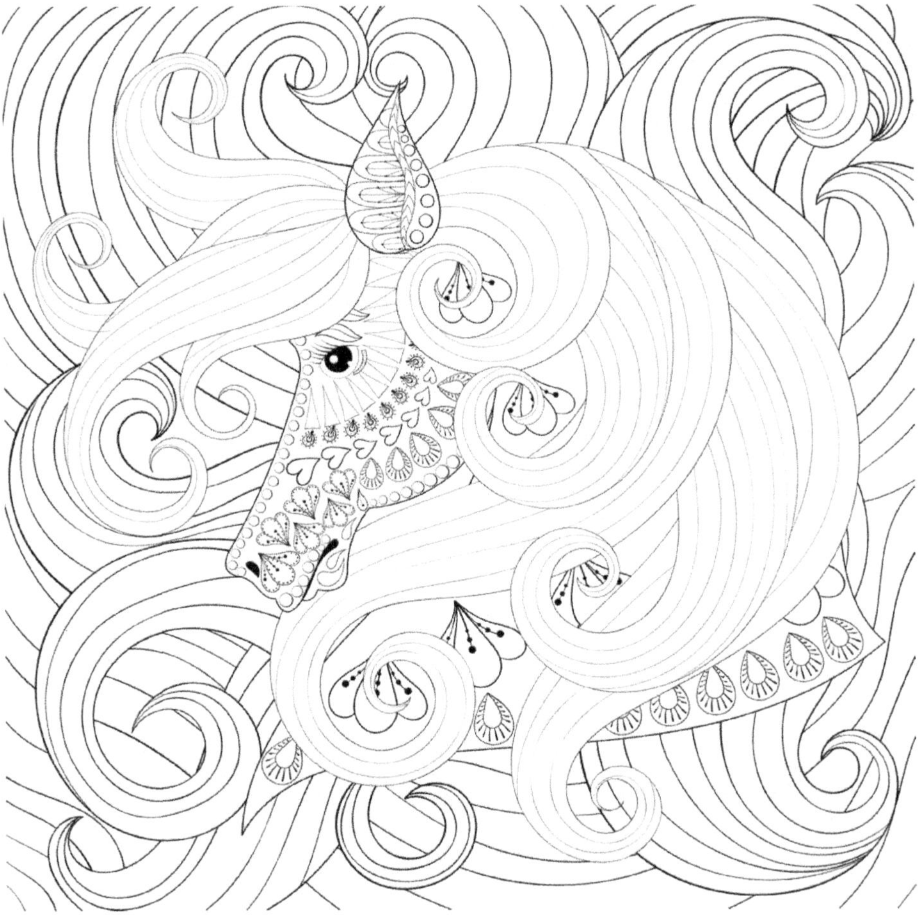

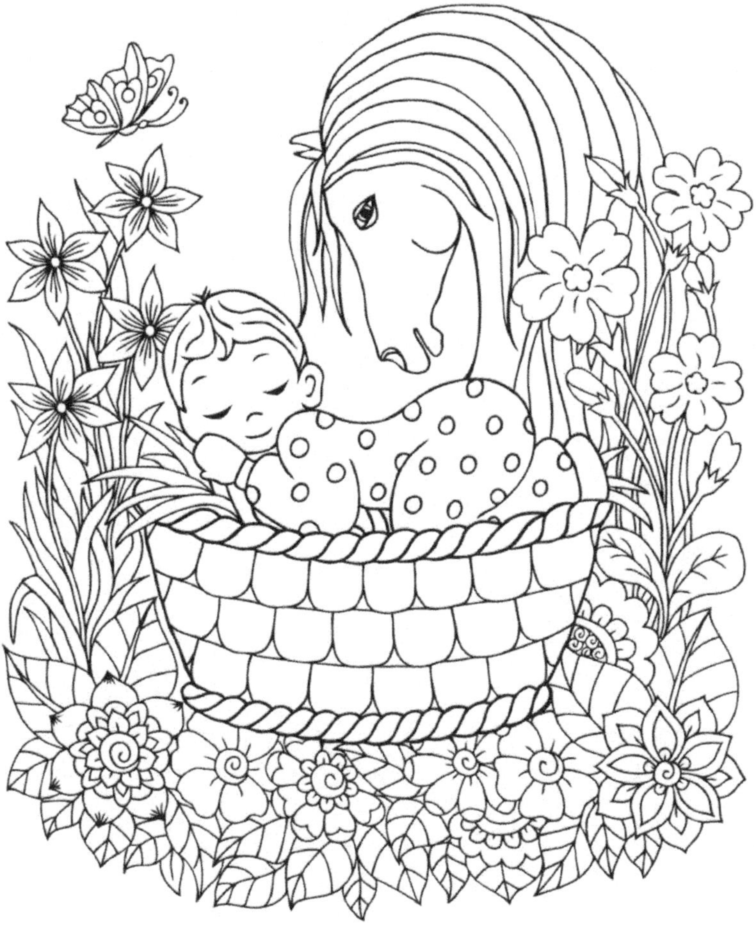

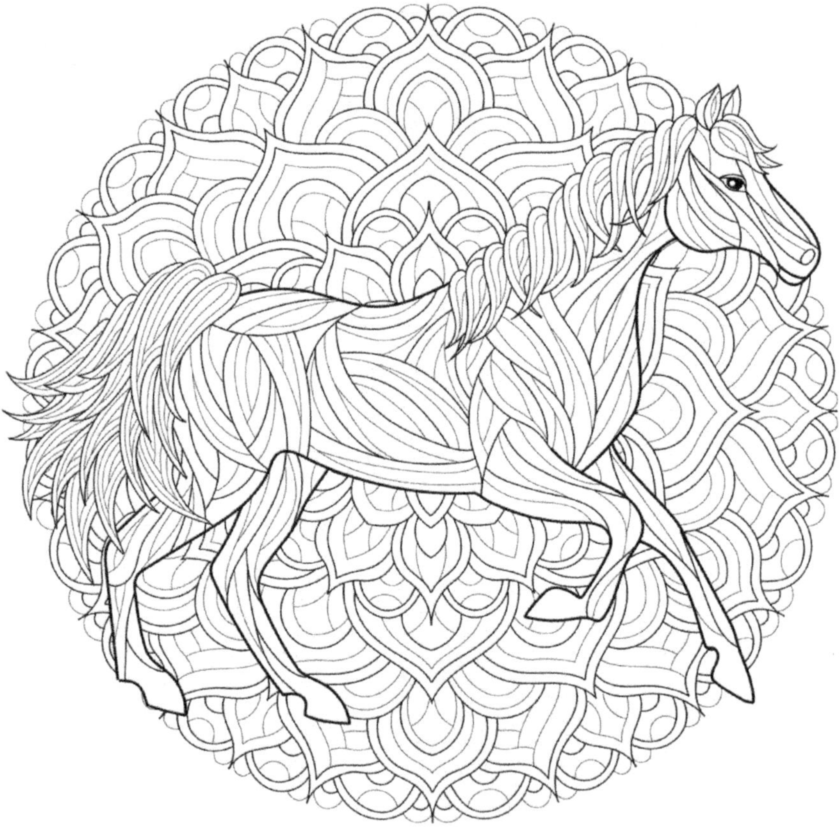

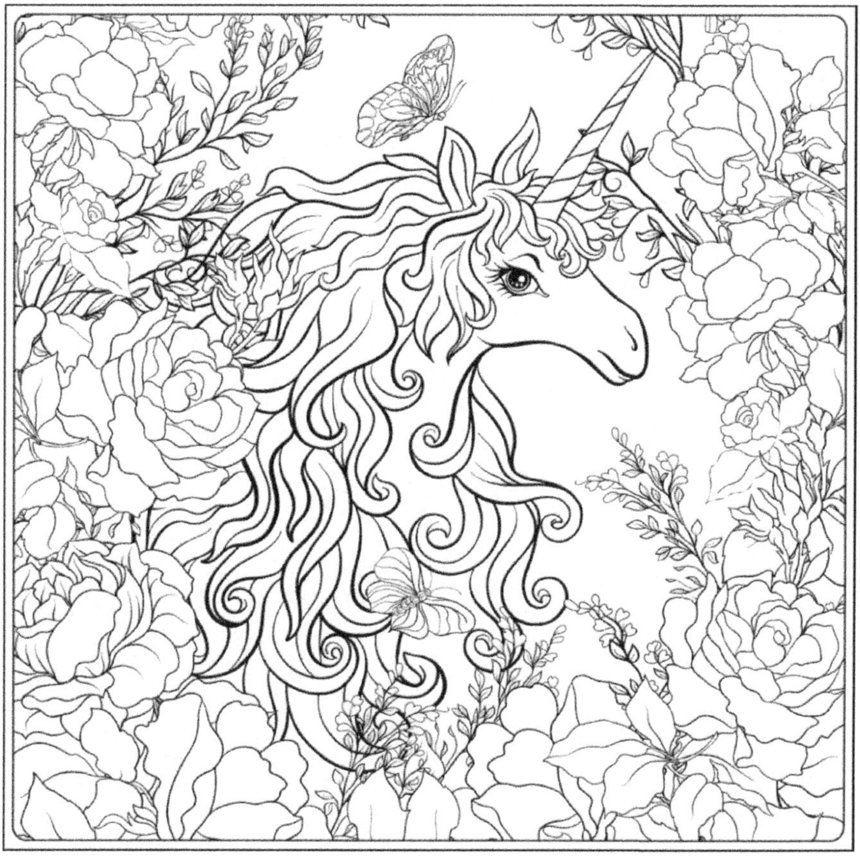

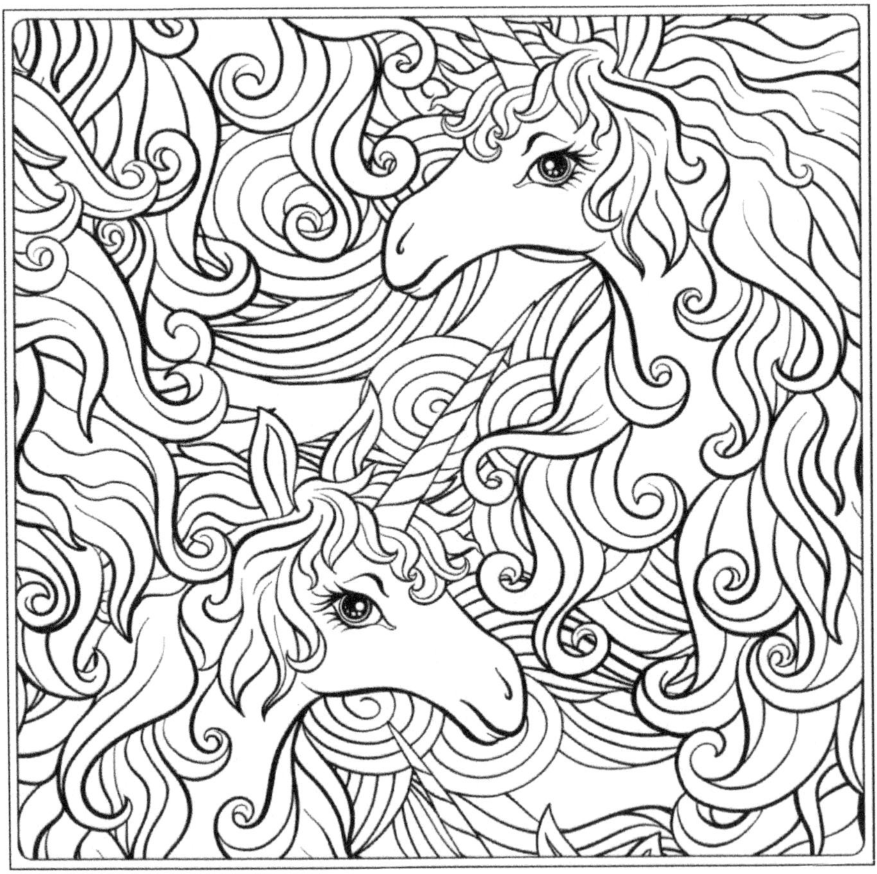

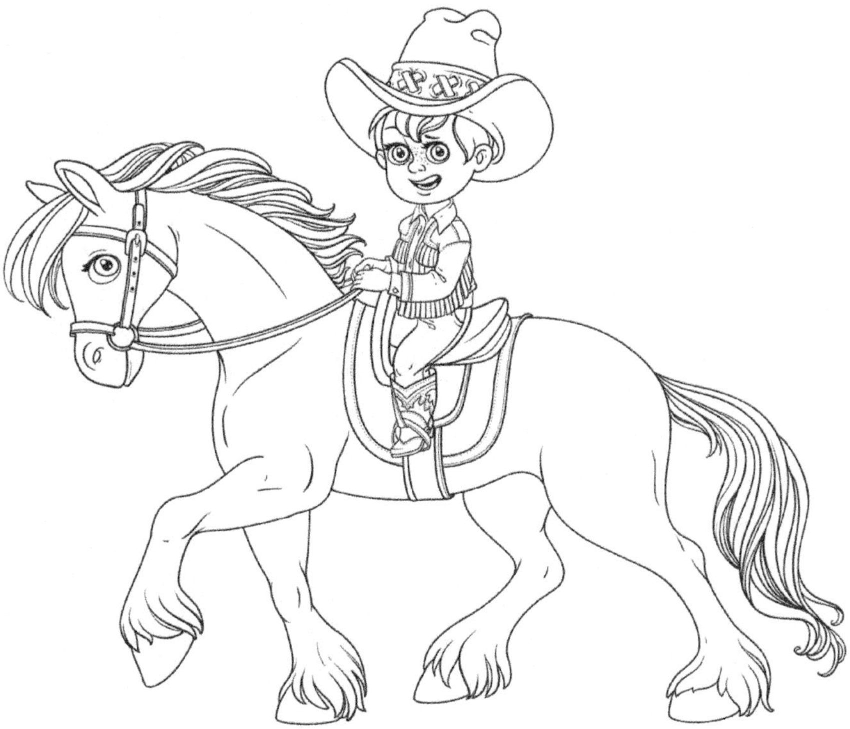

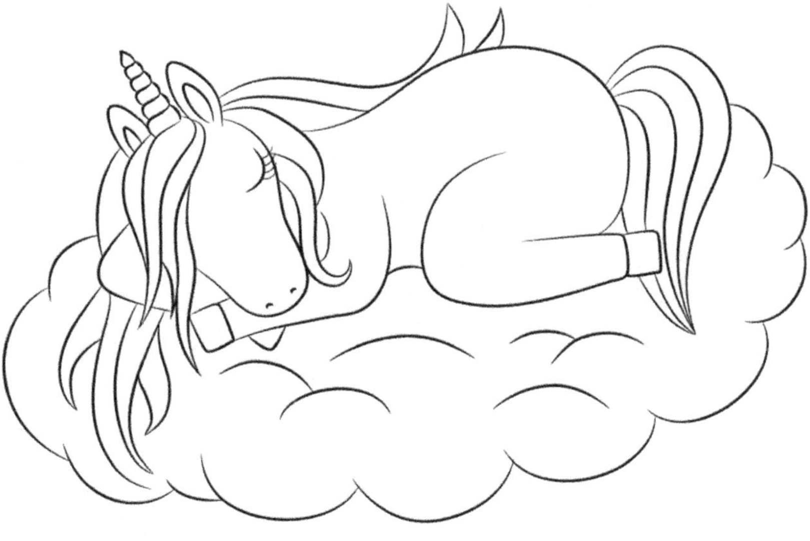

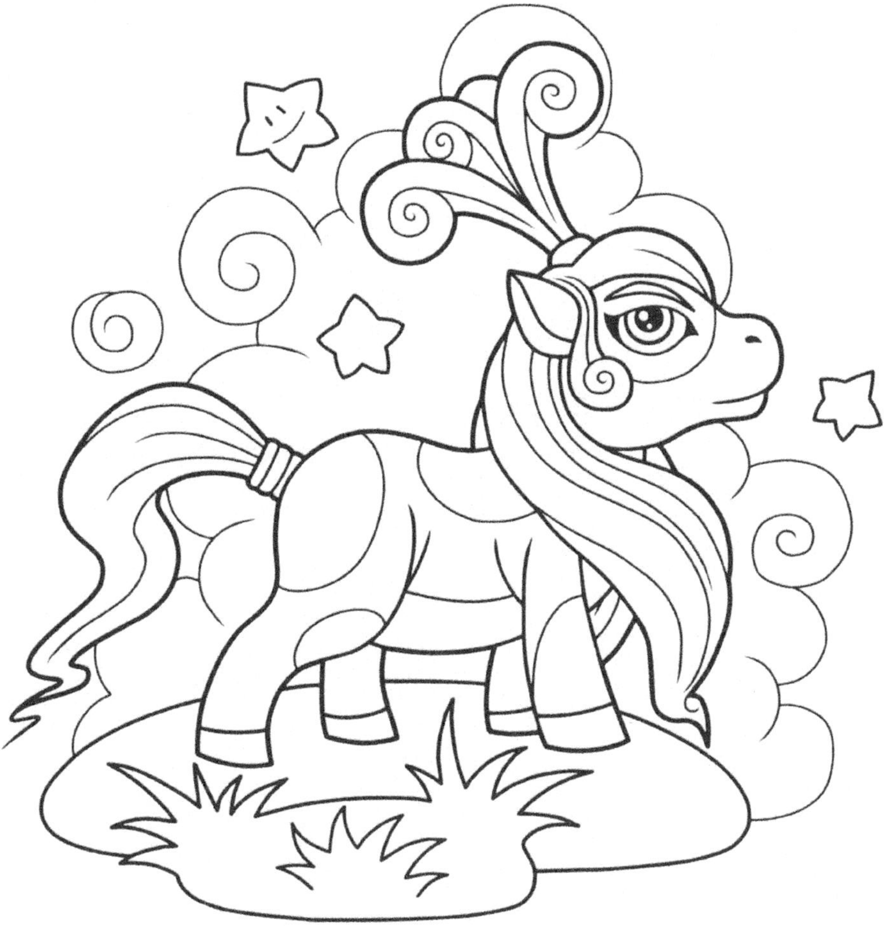

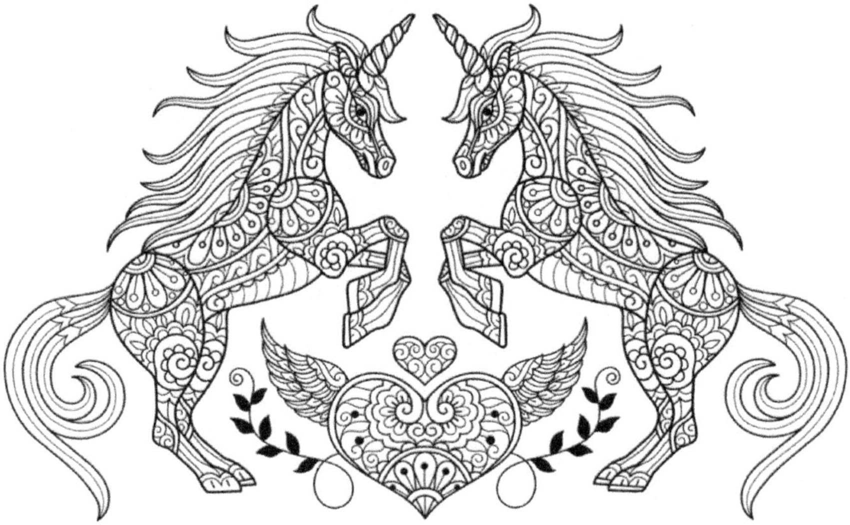

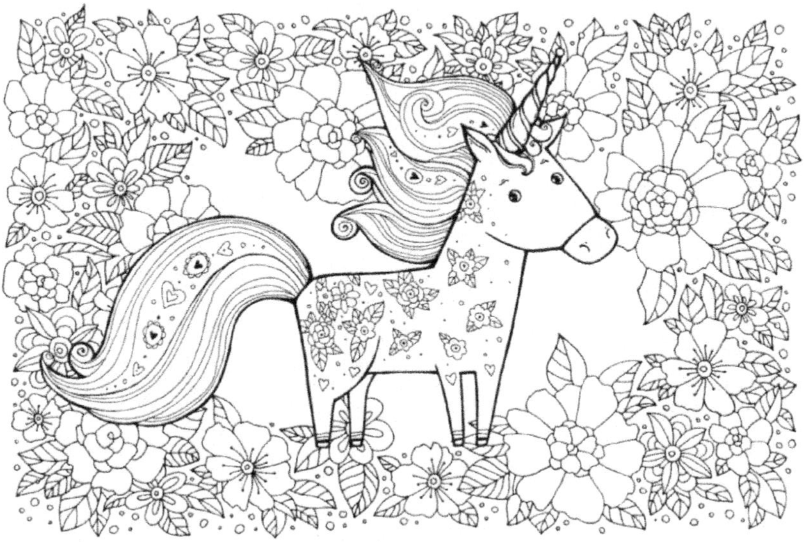

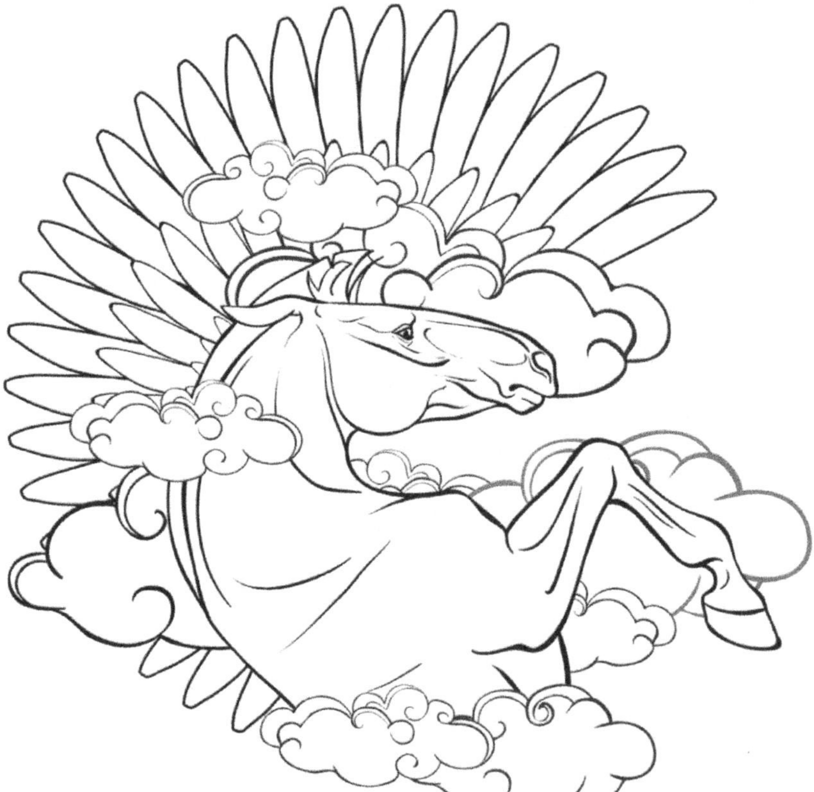

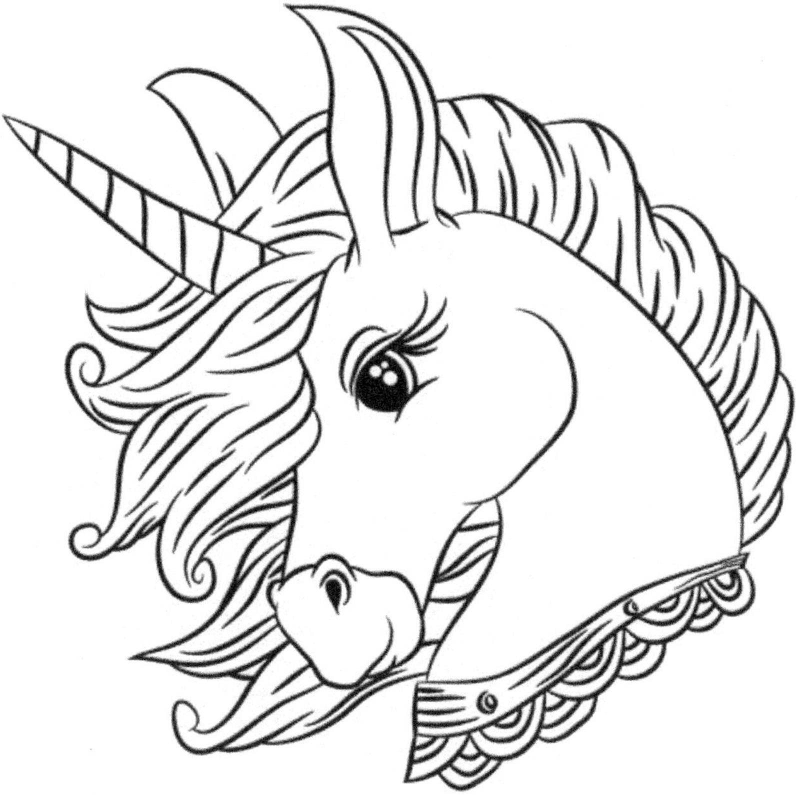

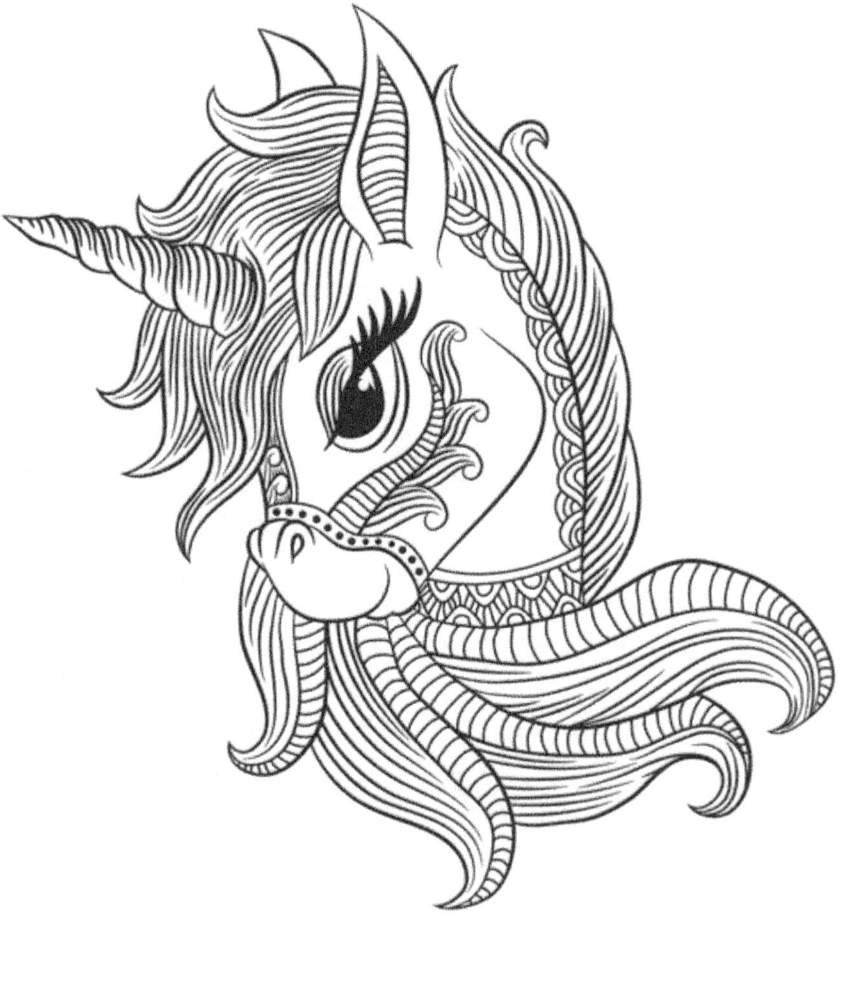

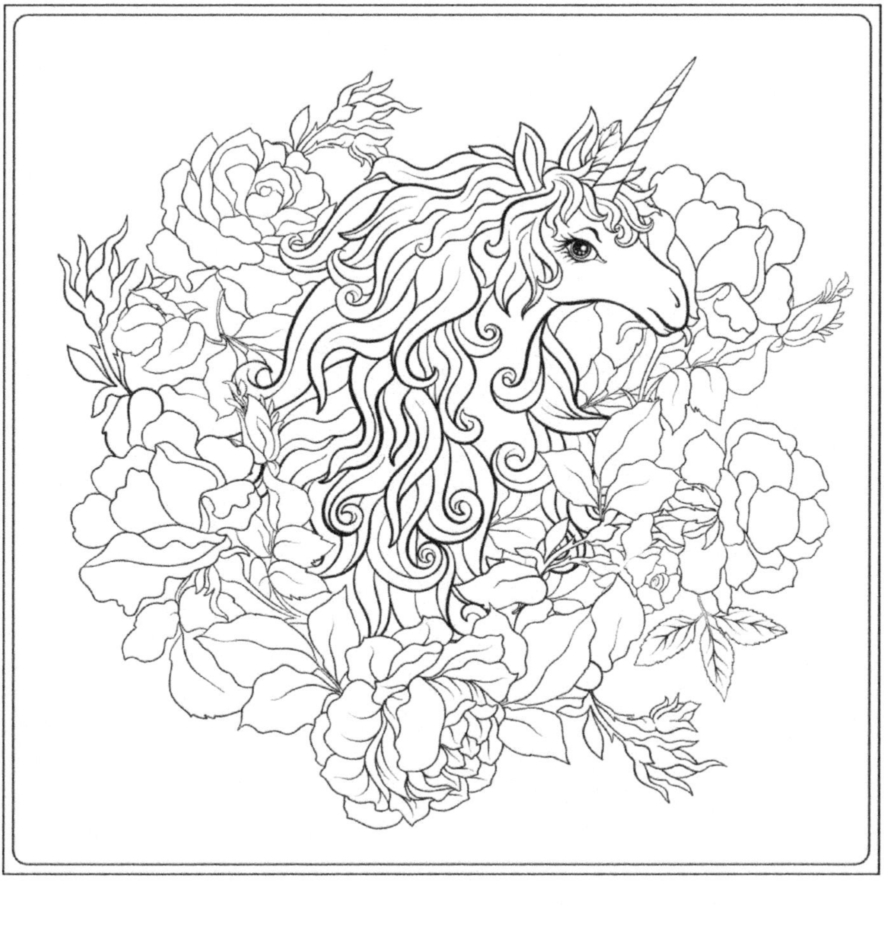

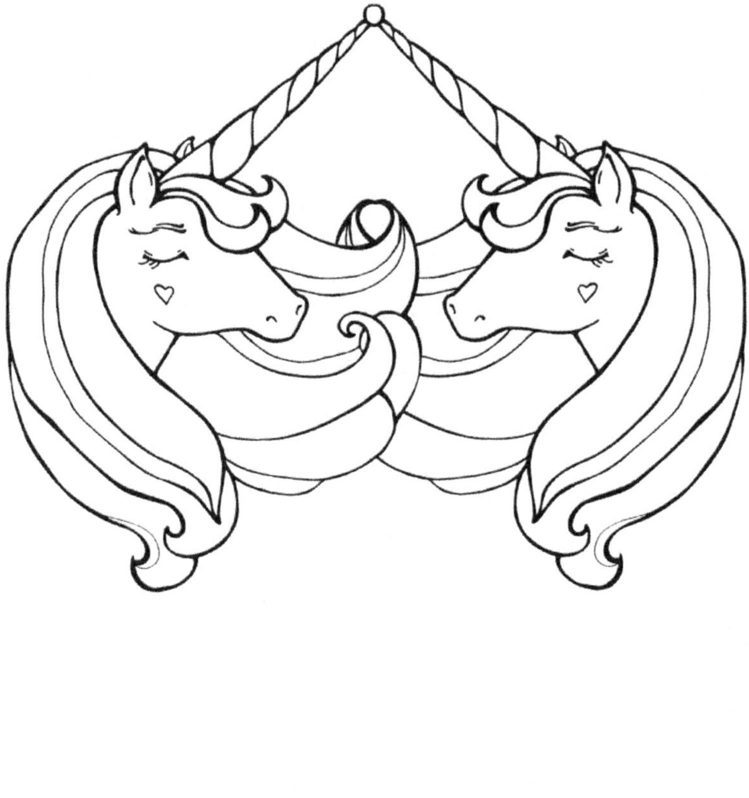

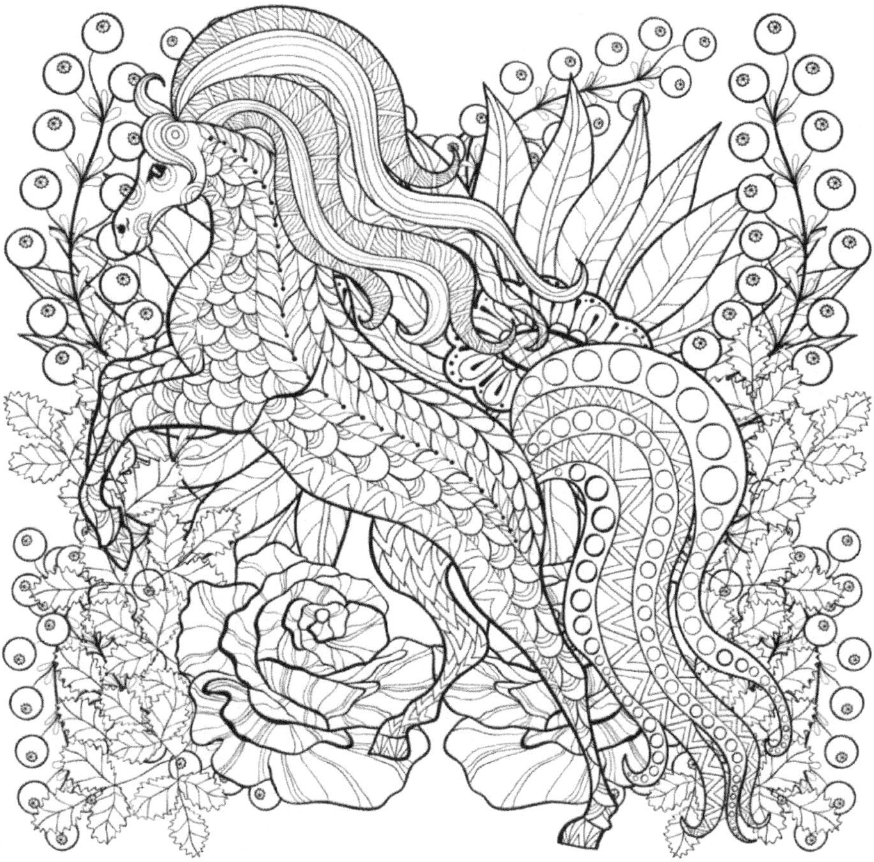

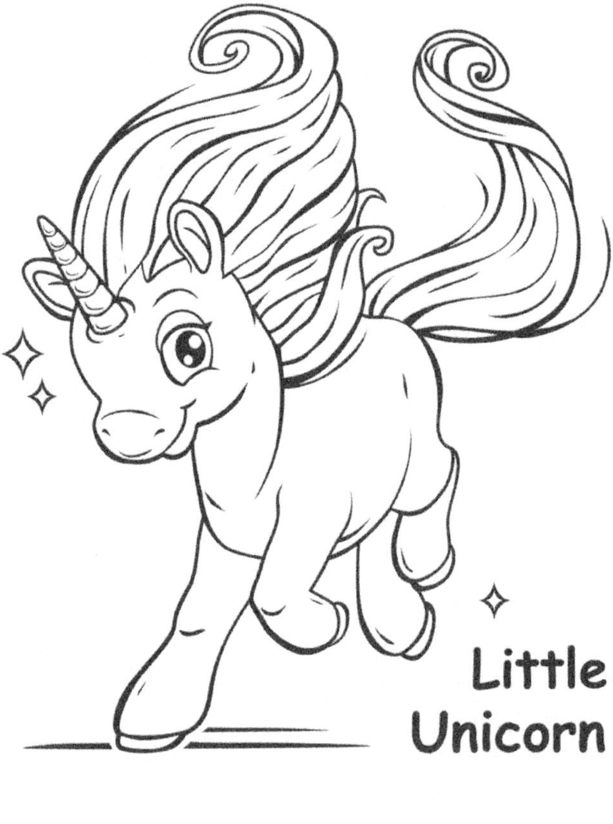

Little
Unicorn

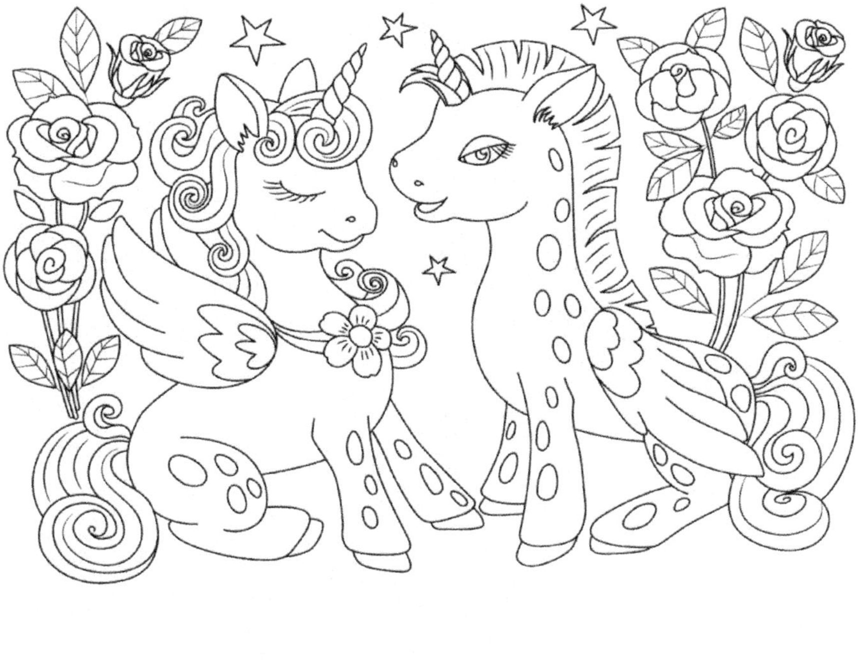

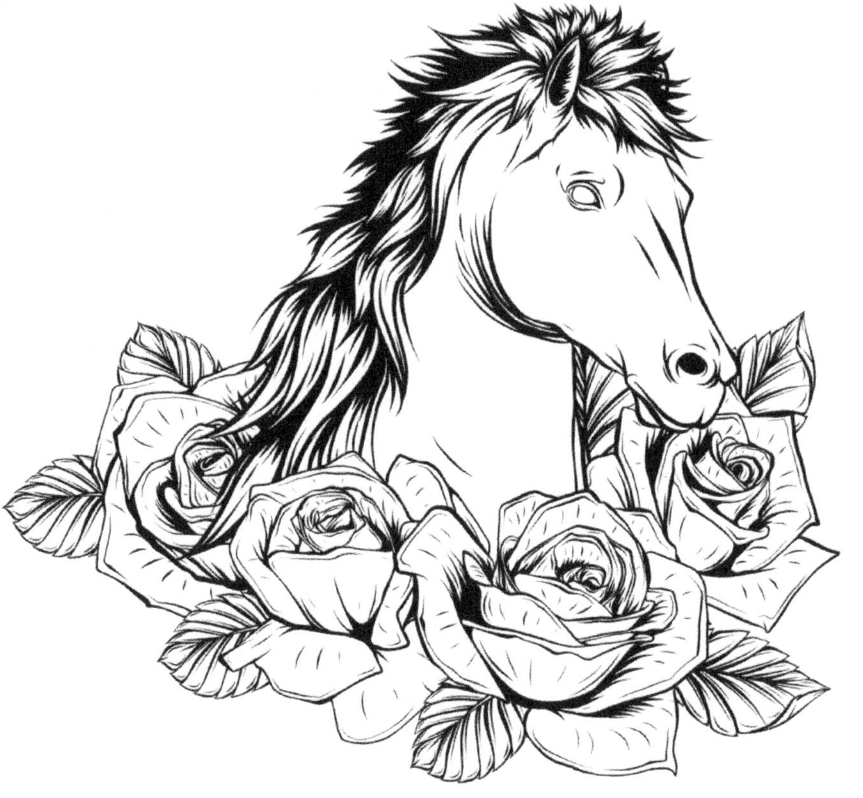

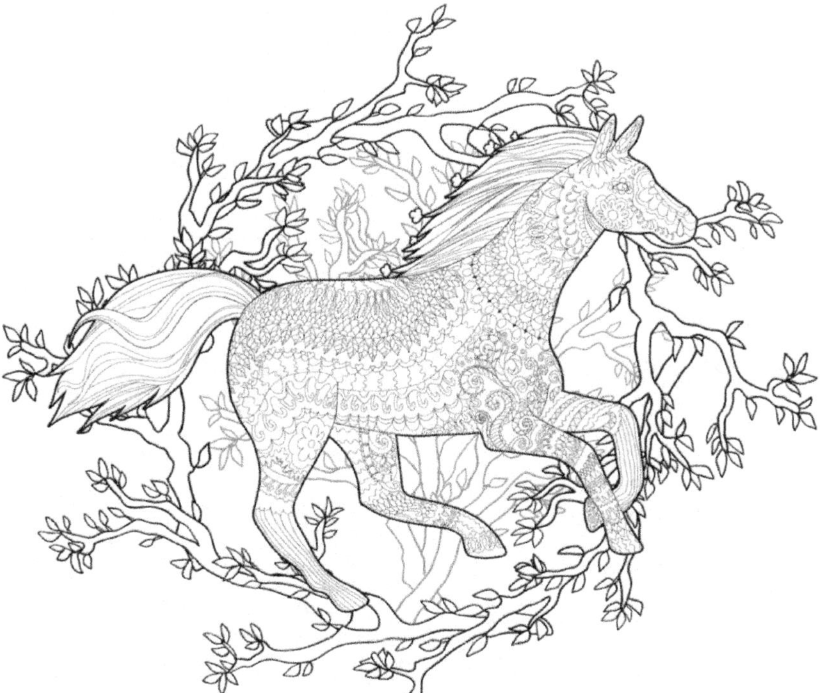

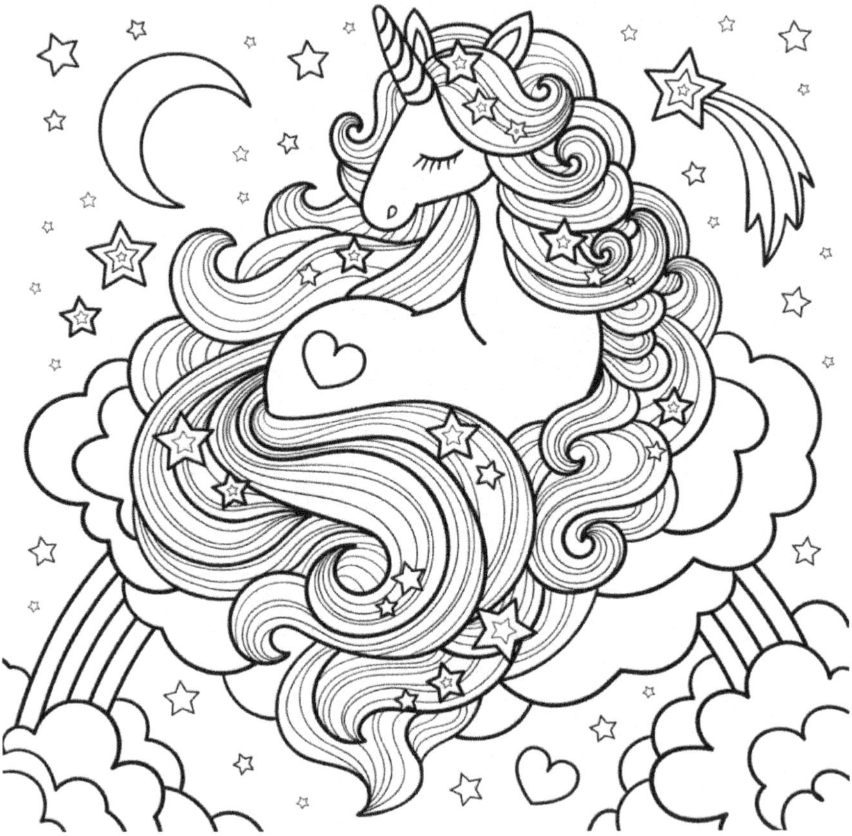

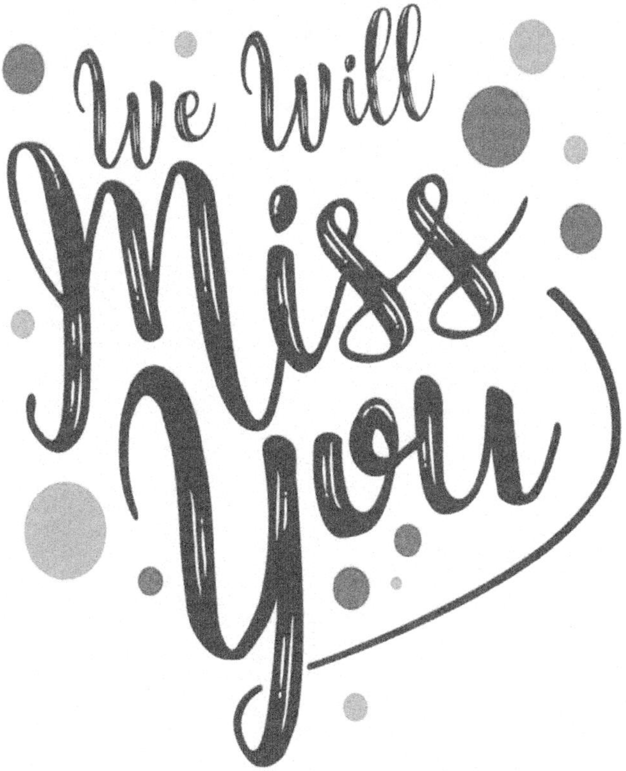
We Will
Miss
You

Made in the USA
Coppell, TX
15 October 2021

64143728R00056